THE ODYSSEY

NOTES

Robert J. Milch
Brooklyn College

Cliffs Notes
INCORPORATED
LINCOLN, NEBRASKA 68501

Editor

Gary Carey, M.A.
University of Colorado

Consulting Editor

James L. Roberts, Ph.D.
Department of English
University of Nebraska

Cliffs Notes, Inc.   Lincoln, Nebraska

CONTENTS

THE ODYSSEY

INTRODUCTION

Odyssey is a Greek word, meaning "the tale of Odysseus." his book, one of the two epics composed by western Europe's rst poet, Homer, is concerned with the adventures and exploits f Odysseus, a hero of the Trojan War.

Reading the *Odyssey* can be a valuable experience for nearly nyone, whether he be a student or a layman. The *Odyssey* is great oetry and one of the foundation stones of the western world's cul- ural heritage. It is also, in a sense, the earliest and one of the finest ooks ever written. It is in the *Odyssey* that the elements of ro- ance and adventure, the psychological development of characters, nd the tight movement of the plot we enjoy so much today were riginated.

Although it is more than 2,500 years old, the *Odyssey* is an easy ook to understand and appreciate, if one is willing to give it a hance. Some parts of this story are strange to people living in the 0th century, but, however odd they seem, it is not difficult to aster them. Study in order to learn about the world in which)dysseus lived and to gain familiarity with the basic material of he tale. Then read the *Odyssey* in full, using some modern trans- ations recommended by your instructor. Do not, by any means, eel that you know the *Odyssey* if you do not read it, for a good tory is made of more than just a bald chain of events. It is also reated by the profound knowledge and understanding of the char- cters that the reader develops and by the unique experience of xposure to the subtle and artistic techniques used by a master toryteller. No outline in the world can provide you with the joy of eading a well-constructed and narrated story. After you have nished the *Odyssey,* reread the outline. It will help to emphasize o you the main points of the epic and will, perhaps, serve to answer ny questions that Homer's work has caused you to ponder.

THE LIFE OF HOMER

Little is known about Homer, the author of the *Iliad* and th
Odyssey and one of the great poets in the history of Western Europe
Ancient Greek tradition, as well as a study of the language and styl
of the poems, indicates that the poet probably lived and wrote some
time in the 8th or 9th centuries B.C., but no more definite date ca
be determined. In ancient times seven different cities claimed th
honor of having been his birthplace. None of these assertions can b
validated, but more than likely he came from the island of Chios, o
the western coast of Asia Minor, for in historical times a family o
the same name lived there which claimed him as an ancestor an
devoted itself to the recitation of his works. Whether or not he di
come from Chios, it is highly probable that he was a native and resi
dent of some section of Asia Minor, for the dialect in which h
composed his works is that of the Asian (Ionian) Greeks.

Tradition has visualized Homer as blind; however, there is n
real evidence for this. This picture is based upon the portrayal o
Demodocus, the blind minstrel in the *Odyssey,* who sings a poen
about the fall of Troy, but there is no reason to believe that th
poet was describing himself in this scene. One scholar has postu
lated that Phemius, the bard in the palace of Ithaca, is Homer'
self-portrait, but again there is no evidence beyond that of one'
own imagination. Throughout the two epics there is consistentl
no autobiographical information and no other literature of the perio
which might describe the poet survives.

The early Greeks unhesitatingly insisted that there had been
single individual named Homer to whom they ascribed the *Iliad*
the *Odyssey,* and several minor works called the *Homeric Hymns*
During the Alexandrian period (after the 3rd century B.C.), wha
is now known as the "Homeric Question" was first propounded
Several of the grammarians of the time asserted that the *Iliad* and
the *Odyssey,* between which there are significant differences of style
and concept, were actually composed by two different writers
This view has at times been supported by later European critics
There has also been a school of thought, originally instituted by

riedrich Wolf in 1795, and especially popular in the 19th century, which claims that Homer never existed and that the two epics are he collective works of groups of anonymous bards to whom the ame Homer was later applied. These scholars suggest that the two oems were constantly revised and added to whenever they were ecited and did not reach their present form until the 6th century .C. when, in Athens, they were written down for the first time.

Contemporary scholarship, in general, believes that each of he two poems has a consistency of style and outlook that shows hem to be the work of one writer. This poet may have composed hem completely or he may have utilized parts of the work of ome earlier bards, altering to fit his own purposes and making hem fully his own in the process. Since the people nearest the composition of the poems believed them to have been the product of ne hand, the modern critic has accepted this view and has attribted the differences between the *Iliad* and the *Odyssey* to their aving been composed in different stages of the poet's life and to he differences in the themes of the works. Rather than take a defensive or apologetic position, the contemporary scholar insists hat the burden of proof is on those who deny the existence of Iomer. To date, this position has not successfully been challenged.

While little if anything is known of Homer's life, his works are n everlasting tribute to him. Progress is an ideal in most fields of uman activity, but in epic poetry it is the two earliest examples which are the best. The *Iliad* and the *Odyssey* have for thousands f years been the standards by which poets of all languages have measured themselves. Homer is magnificent for an understanding of uman nature in all its aspects, for keen observation of the whole world in which men live, for essential sanity and good taste, and for uperb control of all the technical devices of his medium.

THE INFLUENCE OF HOMER

The two epic poems of Homer, the *Iliad* and the *Odyssey,* nust have been recognized as classics soon after their composition, for they had a rapid circulation. By historical times they were known throughout Asia Minor, Greece, and the Greek colonies in the western Mediterranean. The poems were spread by the *rhapsodoi,* professional reciters who traveled through the Greek world, supporting themselves by the presentation of poetry. Such recitations were common, especially at religious festivals and public celebrations. It appears that the poems of Homer were first put into a standard written form by a committee of rhapsodists in Athens, around 535 B.C.

Homer's work was early accepted as the paragon of epic poetry, and his techniques and style were imitated by many later writers. Among the poets who came under his influence was Virgil, a Roman of the 1st Century B.C., whose greatest work was the *Aeneid.* The *Iliad* and *Odyssey* were the common heritage of all Greeks and one of the most important ties binding them together. They soon came to be viewed as sacred, partly because of their great age and beauty, and served for the Greeks very much as the Bible did for the ancient Hebrews. The poems of Homer were accepted as the ultimate authority for information about morality, early history, and the Olympian theology.

With the passing of the ancient world and the triumph of Christianity, the *Iliad* and the *Odyssey* lost their sanctity, but they were still recognized and valued as great poetry. In the medieval period they were forgotten in most of western Europe, but were preserved in Byzantium, where they remained a subject of admiration, imitation, and study. In the 15th century, manuscripts of Homer were brought to Italy from Constantinople. The reintroduction of the *Iliad* and the *Odyssey* was an important factor in the newly emerging humanism of the Renaissance, and since that time these two poems have had a lasting and revered place in the world of literature.

HOMER'S POETIC TECHNIQUE

ORAL POETRY

The *Iliad* and the *Odyssey* are polished epic poems that can easily be classified with the best of any literature. Unlike most ıter poetry, they are the product of a period in which literature was ın oral, unwritten art form. The Greeks of the Homeric period, like ıany other early peoples at a pre-literate level of civilization, pos- essed a kind of heroic poetry which embodied their legends and ıistory, and which was composed, recited, and transmitted orally, ısually by a class of professional bards dedicated to this task.)emodocus and Phemius in the *Odyssey,* who chant old sagas ac- :ompanied by music from their lyres, are representative of these ıards, while the medieval French *Song of Roland* and the *Beowulf* ıaga of Anglo-Saxon Britain are famous non-Greek examples of his heroic poetry.

It is generally believed that Homer was also one of these pro- ıessional bards and that in origin the *Iliad* and the *Odyssey* were ıral works, though probably of greater length than was common for ıuch poems. Since the *Iliad* and the *Odyssey* were probably com- ıosed near the end of Greece's heroic age, there is a possibility hat they were first set down in writing, incorporating parts of earlier ıral poems. This is uncertain, but even if true, writing in this case vould have been used only as an aid to the poet's memory. The style ıf the *Iliad* and the *Odyssey* maintains all of the usual characteristics ıf oral poetry and the poems were obviously meant to be heard, ıot read.

METER

Greek epic poetry was traditionally composed in a meter known ıs the dactylic hexameter. Each hexameter verse has five metrical eet. The first five can consist of a dactyl (a long and two short ıounds, $-(\cup\cup)$ or the first five can consist of a spondee (two long ıounds, $- -$). Whichever method is used the last foot must always ıe a spondee. The number of syllables in a line of hexameter verse ıay vary from a minimum of twelve to a maximum of seventeen, lepending on the combination of dactyls and spondees used.

It often happened that poets had to add extra words to a line to ill it out to the proper number of stresses and accents. It was neces- ıary in such cases that these words, needed only to fulfill the metrical equirements of the hexameter, should not confuse or change the ıeaning of the verse, and for this purpose the poets devised the epithet, a conventional word or phrase which was attached to a noun (whether person, place or thing) and which could be added when needed without affecting the meaning of the sentence or phrase in which it was used.

EPITHETS

To the modern reader, who finds the *Iliad* and the *Odyssey* in an English translation and is unfamiliar with the technical require ments of the hexameter, which necessitated the use of conventional extra words, the epithet appears only as a sometimes confusing sometimes meaningful, stock word or short phrase regularly applied to some person or thing. Typical epithets used in the *Odyssey* in clude "rosy-fingered dawn," "bright-eyed Athene," "sandy Pylos," and "wise Odysseus." Besides their technical function, epithets are a useful stylistic device, helping the audience better to visualize what is being narrated and aiding the poet in making concise char acterizations or descriptions. In the hands of Homer the traditional epithet was also used to achieve brilliant effects of irony and under statement, by his contrasting of the meaning of a traditional epithet with the real nature of the person or thing to which it was applied. A good example of the way Homer does this is his frequent applica tion of the epithet "brave" to the craven and wicked Antinous, leader of Penelope's suitors.

SIMILES

The most prevalent form of imagery used in the *Iliad* and the *Odyssey* is the simile, a poetic comparison of an individual, thing, or event to something else of greater familiarity to the audience. A typical Homeric simile is this one in which the starving Odysseus is described as he emerges from behind some bushes to confront Nausicaa and her maids (*Odyssey,* Book VI):

> Then he advanced on them like a mountain lion who sallies out, defying wind and rain in the pride of his power, with fire in his eyes, to hunt the oxen or the sheep, to stalk the roaming deer, or to be forced by hunger to besiege the very walls of the homestead and attack the pens. The same urgent need now constrained

Odysseus, naked as he was, to bear down upon these
gentle girls.

By making his comparisons with the objects and experiences of
everyday life, Homer not only made the heroic content of his poem
far more understandable to his audience, but also created some fine
effects of contrast and some short lyrical passages of great beauty.

FORMAL RHETORIC

A great part of the *Odyssey* is made up of long, formal speeches
by the characters, even in scenes which are meant to include conversation. This is because shorter, more realistic dialogue would
have been difficult to recite and hard to understand in an oral presentation. In addition, the stateliness of the oratory composed by
Homer adds to the dignity of his story and helps to counteract the
more fabulous aspects of some of its episodes. Throughout their
history, the Greeks had a great fondness for public speaking and
viewed oratory as a practical communications medium and also as
a creative art form. To a great extent this was because of the author-
itative example set by Homer in the *Iliad* and the *Odyssey*.

REPETITION

Modern readers quickly notice another characteristic feature of
oral poetry — the frequent repetition of epithets, similes, speeches,
and episodes. Such repetition is typical of oral poetry for obvious
reasons — it reduced the difficulties of composition and made the
poem easier to memorize. In addition, repetition helped refresh the
memories of listeners during recitations and enabled them to recognize or anticipate certain developments or kinds of action. Since
poems as long as the *Odyssey* were too long to be recited in a single
session, such repetition would have been more helpful and less dis-
tracting to an ancient audience than to a modern reader.

LANGUAGE

The language in which the Homeric poems are composed is an
artificial literary dialect with many archaic elements, comparable in
this regard to the language used by the translators of the King James
version of the Bible. The language of the *Odyssey* is basically a form

of the Ionian dialect of Greek spoken in Asia Minor and Attica, bu
has many Aeolian words and constructions.

GENERAL COMMENT

Although many aspects of Greek epic technique were traditional and did not originate with Homer, he brought a new spirit and
skill to their use. It was natural for him to do his work in the style
already developed and accepted in his society. In the same manner
all writers and poets have worked within the framework prepared
for them by their predecessors. The best of them, like Homer, have
surpassed the tools with which they were provided and have molded
the conventional forms they inherited into unique and highly personal modes of artistic expression.

LIST OF CHARACTERS

HUMAN BEINGS

Alcinous	Melanthius
Antinous	Melantho
Arete	Menelaus
Demodocus	Mentor
Elpenor	Nausicaa
Eumaeus	Nestor
Eurycleia	Odysseus
Eurylochus	Peisistratus
Eurymachus	Penelope
Halisthernes	Philoetius
Helen	Telemachus
Irus	Theoclymenus
Laertes	Tiresias
Medon	

GODS AND SUPERNATURAL BEINGS

Aeolus	Charybdis
Athene	Circe
Calypso	Hermes

Hyperion   Scylla
Leucothoie   The Sirens
Polyphemus   Zeus
Poseidon

SYNOPSIS OF THE *ODYSSEY*

Odysseus, king of Ithaca, sails with his army to take part in the ighty Achaean expedition led by Agamemnon against the city of roy to restore Helen to Menelaus. After ten years of bloody war- re, the city is sacked and the Achaean heroes sail for home. 'hen the *Odyssey* begins, an additional decade has passed since roy fell and Odysseus still has not returned home. All the other iieftains have safely arrived in their native lands or died, but there no news at all of the ruler of Ithaca. In his absence, the noblemen ' Ithaca and the surrounding states have converged upon his palace, ping to win the hand of Penelope, his wife. She, ever faithful to r husband's memory, will not remarry and while they remain at e palace, trying to change her mind, the suitors grossly waste e wealth of Odysseus' estate for their own pleasure and corrupt any of his servants. As soon as he has grown old enough, Telem- :hus, the son of Odysseus, visits various Achaean lords, hopefully ying to learn whether his father still lives.

During these ten years Odysseus has wandered throughout the orld, undergoing an unbelievable series of adventures and tor- ents, caused by the malice of the god, Poseidon. All his ships and en have been lost and only he of the whole brave army that sailed Troy survives. Finally, with the aid of the king of the Phaeacians, dysseus returns to Ithaca. Assisted by the goddess Athene, whose vorite he is, Odysseus punishes the suitors and re-establishes imself as king. He is reunited with his wife, son and father, and a otential civil war on Ithaca is averted by the intercession of e gods.

SUMMARIES AND COMMENTARIES

BOOK I

ATHENE ADVISES TELEMACHUS

Summary

The *Odyssey* opens with Homer's invocation to the muse of poetry, in which he states the subject of the epic and asks for her guidance in telling his story properly. It is, he says, the tale of a lonely man who has wandered throughout the world for many years and who has suffered many hardships before his attempt to return home was successful.

When the story proper begins, all the survivors of the Trojan War have safely reached their homes, with the exception of Odysseus. He is being detained by the nymph Calypso, who hopes to make him her husband, and while most of the gods are sympathetic to him, Poseidon, ruler of the sea, bears him a grudge and makes him undergo many torments.

In the absence of Poseidon, a divine council is called on Olympus by Zeus, the king of the gods. After his introductory speech about the punishment of Aegisthus, the murderer of Agamemnon, Athene interrupts her father. She reminds him of poor Odysseus, separated from family and loved ones on a distant island, and demands that the gods resume their former friendship to him. She points out that while Poseidon is bitter because Odysseus has blinded one of his sons, yet he can still be made to submit to the combined will of the other gods. She suggests that Hermes be sent to Calypso, ordering her to free Odysseus, while she will disguise herself and go to see Telemachus, the son of Odysseus. Zeus and the other gods agree to this suggestion.

Athene outfits herself as a mighty warrior and goes at once to Ithaca, the home of Odysseus. There she finds the hero's house overrun by a horde of petty princes and young noblemen who are

tensibly courting his wife, but who are, at the same time, having
constant series of banquets and feasts at which they waste all of
dysseus' property.

Athene, identifying herself as Mentes, a Taphian chieftain and
old friend of Odysseus, is welcomed by Telemachus. The two
t down to dinner and the young man apologizes for the crude
havior of the suitors. He asks Athene for news of his father,
any. Athene reassures Telemachus that Odysseus is still alive
mewhere and that he will eventually return home to recognize his
n and punish the suitors. Telemachus describes the problems
used by his father's absence and explains how Penelope, his
other, has refused to remarry. Athene recommends that Tele-
achus call a meeting of the Assembly at which he can give the
itors notice to leave his house and can at the same time announce
s intention of seeking news of Odysseus. Then, the goddess ad-
ses, he should sail for Pylos and Sparta to learn what he can from
estor and Menelaus. Furthermore, Athene points out, if Odysseus
dead, then it is time for Telemachus to face his responsibilities,
claiming his inheritance, having his mother select a new husband,
d by punishing the suitors. The goddess leaves, and the two part
friends.

Meanwhile, at the banquet of the suitors, a bard sings of the
ventures of the Achaeans at Troy. Penelope appears and is upset
this reminder of the long absent Odysseus, but Telemachus orders
r to leave the hall, where the entertainment is, after all, for men
d not for sensitive women. The suitors then attempt to question
e youth about his recent guest. He announces that he will call
e Assembly the next morning as well as his planned voyage in
est of information and his intended punishment of them all.
hey are surprised at his sudden assertion of manliness, but con-
ue with their wasteful feasting. Telemachus goes to bed and
eams of his impending journey.

ommentary

The *Odyssey*, like all epics, begins with an invocation to the
use of poetry in which Homer announces the theme of his poem
d asks for divine assistance in telling the story. The custom of

invoking the muse is based on an ancient belief that the ability t
create poetry, which was also thought of as the ability to give a kin
of immortality to the people whose stories were told in the poen
was a mysterious and godlike art that could only be practiced wit
supernatural help.

The method of storytelling in ancient Greece was very diffe
ent from our own and this is reflected in Homer's narrative style i
the *Odyssey*. Greek epic poems told stories about things whic
had taken place in the legendary past and which were believed b
the Greeks to be historical, so the details of the stories, or at lea
their general outlines, were already well known. Because of this th
epic poet could not use many of the storytelling devices that ar
common today, such as the surprise ending or the development (
suspense. He concentrated on interpretation and explication of th
old tales and on achieving a high level of artistry in retelling then

Since his audience was already familiar with the story told i
his poem, Homer was able to omit many unimportant details in
cluded in the original legends and could start the *Odyssey* at a mor
dramatic point in the story than its chronological beginning. No sun
mary of earlier events was necessary and he did not have to intro
duce or give the backgrounds of his characters. This technique
which is characteristic of all epic poetry, is known as starting i
medias res (a Latin phrase meaning "in the middle of things"
It serves immediately to capture the attention of the audience at th
beginning of a recitation. In conjunction with this technique, back
ground information and the story of the first nine years of th
wanderings of Odysseus are presented by use of flashbacks a
points in the poem where they have added meaning or a more strik
ing effect. This helps to make the poem more dramatic and tighten
the integration of the many diverse elements of its plot, so that, a
a narrative poem, the *Odyssey's* plot has much more unity than th
more loosely organized plot of the *Iliad*.

Although the *Iliad* and *Odyssey* have many features in common
there are some significant differences between the two epics. On
immediately apparent even in the first book and fundamental to th
entire mood of the *Odyssey,* is that it contains much less historica

material than the *Iliad* and gives greater weight to magic and other supernatural phenomena. The ancient legends and traditions on which the *Iliad* is based are supported by the findings of archeology and have a foundation in real history. There is little evidence for a settlement in Mycenaean times on Ithaca, the home island of Odysseus, and most of the other places he is supposed to have visited cannot be identified. The scholarly consensus is that most of the poem's episodes have little or no historical basis. Moreover, common folklore motifs which are not typical of Greek legend, such as monsters and witches (e.g., Polyphemus the Cyclops and Circe), abound in the *Odyssey*. For these reasons most scholars believe that the main sources of the *Odyssey* are to be found in the realm of folklore, fairy tale, and travelers' yarns, in which the supernatural usually plays a great part. There may once have been a real chieftain named Odysseus to whom these stories somehow became attached, but most of the tales are far more ancient than the time in which he is supposed to have lived, and parallels to them can be found in the folk-literatures of many different periods in places ranging from Asia to western Europe.

Three main themes have been harmonized into a single story with the result that the *Odyssey* has an intricately constructed and highly unified plot. The three main themes are:

1. "The Wanderings of Odysseus" which consists mainly of folklore elements, though perhaps it is based partially on some vague historical memories. ("The Wanderings of Menelaus" in Book IV is thought to be an ancient variant of the same legendary theme simply using a different hero..

2. "The Quest of Telemachus" which is known to scholars as the *Telemacheia*, occupies most of Books I-IV and sections of later books. As an account of the maturation and education of a young man (a *bildungsroman*) it is unique in Greek literature.

3. "The Return and Vengeance" was originally folklore. It begins where the "Wanderings" end, although the two are bound together by the indirect form of narrative and the many flashbacks used throughout the *Odyssey*.

Originally all of these themes may have been independen[t] stories or collections of stories that Homer revised and unified b[y] the introduction of the character of Odysseus. The skillful orga[n]ization of so many diverse elements into one story and the consta[nt] emphasis on the experiences of a single man is important. Man[y] critics have described the *Odyssey* as the first novel ever writte[n] and have considered the Odyssey to be the prototype of all romant[ic] literature in the western world.

BOOK II

THE ASSEMBLY OF ITHACA MEETS

Summary

In the morning, Telemachus dresses and grooms himself wit[h] great care and orders the heralds to call the men of Ithaca to th[e] Assembly. At the meeting, Aegyptius, one of the old chieftain[s] expresses his pleasure at discovering that a meeting has been co[n]vened after such a long lapse, for this is the first session of th[e] Assembly since Odysseus and the army sailed for Troy 19 yea[rs] before.

Telemachus takes the speaker's staff and declares that he ha[s] called the meeting not because of any matter of civic danger [or] necessity, but to officially denounce the scoundrels who are wastin[g] his father's wealth on the pretext of courting his mother. He poin[ts] out that Odysseus, were he present, would punish them severel[y] In addition, Telemachus says, he would punish them himself if h[e] were ever powerful enough. The gathered Assembly is silent i[n] shame and pity for a few moments, but then Telemachus is attacke[d] vehemently by Antinous, one of the most insolent of the suitors. H[e] arrogantly denies all guilt and places the blame on Penelope, wh[o] he says, has led the suitors on, but refused to choose one of the[m] thus preventing them from selecting other wives.

Telemachus repeats his threats to punish the suitors and tw[o] eagles of Zeus appear in the sky to emphasize his remarks. Hali[s]thernes the soothsayer reminds the Assembly that he has predicte[d] all these events, including the return of Odysseus within the coming year. He points out that in the past his prophecies have all been true and sternly warns them to take heed. Eurymachus, another suitor, accuses the old seer of accepting bribes from Telemachus and berates his prophecies. He also adds that the suitors will not leave until Penelope has selected one of them. Telemachus then proposes that he be given a ship and crew to seek news of Odysseus. He asserts that if his father is really dead, he will conduct a funeral ceremony and guarantee that his mother will choose another husband, but, if his father is alive somewhere, he will submit to no more than one more year of the suitors' profligacy. An old friend of Odysseus, Mentor, rises to speak and praises the wisdom of the young man, but other suitors harangue him and the Assembly disperses without further action.

At the seashore, Telemachus prays to Athene for help. She appears to him disguised as Mentor and together they plan to get a ship despite the opposition of the suitors. Telemachus returns home, where he engages in an argument with Antinous, after which the other suitors mock him and his hopes. The youth tells his old nurse, Eurycleia, of his plans and with her aid he secretly removes supplies for the trip from the storerooms. He orders her to keep knowledge of the journey from Penelope for as long as possible so that she will not worry about him.

At the same time, Athene, disguised now as Telemachus, roams through the town organizing a crew of twenty young men and procuring a ship. Returning to the appearance of Mentor, the goddess joins Telemachus and they, with the crew, load the ship. As night falls they set sails on the first leg of the voyage to Pylos.

Commentary

The meeting of the Assembly of Ithaca in this book illustrates a feature of political organization in Homeric times which was derived from the tribal structure of the Indo-European peoples who invaded Greece in the second millenium B.C., and is the source of the political institutions which eventually developed into the democratic governments of Athens and other Greek city-states in historical times. Homeric kings were not absolute rulers, but were subject to laws and traditions and to the criticism of their peers. In the Homeric state important changes or innovations in governmental policy had to be presented to an assembly of all the male citizens. This assembly could not initiate discussion or convene itself, but it had the right to approve or disapprove steps suggested to it. Because of this, members of the ruling class had always to keep in mind the opinions, desires, and interests of the people. This heritage of popular participation in government is one of the most important Greek contributions to western civilization.

One of the interesting unsolved historical problems of the *Odyssey* is why doesn't Telemachus become king of Ithaca? Why does not Laertes, the father of Odysseus, come out of retirement to take over the reins of government and save Penelope from all her difficulties with the suitors? Why don't people of Ithaca rise to protect their queen. There are two possible answers: (1) that Telemachus cannot become king unless the Assembly elects him and he does not yet have enough prestige to put himself to this test, while the people, being without a ruler, have no one to give them orders and (2) more likely in view of the efforts of the suitors to win Penelope in marriage, Ithaca was once a matriarchal society and descent is still determined through the female not the male line, so that Odysseus is king because he married Penelope, the hereditary queen, and not, as is elsewhere assumed in the poem, because he inherited the kingdom from his father. This would explain why Telemachus, the son of the queen, and Laertes, the husband of the dead former queen, have no claims on the throne. Such matriarchal organization was common among many primitive peoples and existed in Greece before the advent of the Indo-European patriarchal tribes. In Homeric times Greece no longer had a matriarchal system, but many old customs and beliefs still survived. In all probability, the legend which Homer adapted for use in the *Odyssey* was pre-Indo-European in origin and still contained some matriarchal elements which were no longer understood. That is why there is never any clear explanation of this confusing situation in the *Odyssey* and that also explains why there are some patriarchal customs and viewpoints mixed into the story.

BOOK III

TELEMACHUS AND NESTOR

Summary

When Telemachus, accompanied by Athene in the guise of
Mentor, reaches Pylos, he finds King Nestor with his sons and
retainers on the beach, offering nine bulls in sacrifice to Poseidon.
The pair are received graciously, and are invited to partake of the
ritual dinner which is about to begin.

After eating, the two identify themselves, and Telemachus
explains the nature of his mission. Old Nestor, in his usual verbose
fashion, describes the last days of the Trojan expedition. After the
city fell, he says, a dispute occurred between Agamemnon, the
commander, and his brother, Menelaus. The army divided into
two factions and these sailed for home separately. Odysseus had
put out from Troy with Nestor, along with Diomedes and others,
but another quarrel took place at Tenedos, and Odysseus left this
squadron to rejoin Agamemnon. This was the last that Nestor
knew for sure of the father of Telemachus, although since then he
had heard that he had not yet returned to Ithaca. The aged chieftain
rambles on to tell of the arrivals home of the other heroes, of the
murder of Agamemnon by Aegisthus, his wife's seducer, and the
punishment of the killer by Orestes. He goes on to recount the
wanderings of Menelaus, whom a storm blew to Egypt, and who
had only recently returned to his kingdom, after many adventures
and with much newly acquired wealth. Nestor suggests that
Telemachus consult Menelaus since he may have more recent
information. Telemachus and Mentor agree that this is a wise idea.
After further conversation, Nestor invites the young man to spend
the night in his palace. Telemachus does so.

In the morning, sacrifice is made to Athene. Then Nestor
supplies Telemachus with a chariot so that he can travel to Sparta
to speak with Menelaus. Accompanied by Peisistratus, Nestor's
youngest son, the heir of Odysseus continues on his journey.

Commentary

Nestor, the king of Pylos, was the oldest and wisest of the Achaeans at Troy and a good friend of Odysseus, so he is obviously the first one to turn to for information and advice. His account of the sailing of the fleet from Troy is the first mention of the adventures of Odysseus during the nine years between the fall of the city and his arrival on Calypso's island, where he was said to be in Book I. The way in which the story of the adventures of Odysseus is told illustrates Homer's sense of drama and lack of concern for chronology — first, this part of the story is told, then, in Book V — Odysseus appears on Calypso's island in the ninth year of his wanderings, then, in Book IX — during the tenth year, Odysseus himself tells about his adventures during the first nine, and then, with the background completely filled in, his story continues on Ithaca in the tenth year.

Throughout the *Odyssey* Homer contrasts the legend about the homecoming of Agamemnon with the story of Odysseus. Some parts of the legend are told to Telemachus by Nestor, more will be told by Menelaus in the next book, and the remainder will be told by Agamemnon himself when Odysseus visits Hades (Book XI). Briefly, the legend is as follows: While Agamemnon, the king of Mycenae and chief of the Achaean forces, was away at Troy, he left his cousin Aegisthus as regent in his place. During Agamemnon's absence, Aegisthus seduced his wife Clytemnestra. The two lovers plotted to kill Agamemnon when he returned home so they could marry and take over the government. Immediately following Agamemnon's triumphal entry into Mycenae after the war, they murdered him. Eventually Orestes, the son of Agamemnon, avenged his father by killing Aegisthus and Clytemnestra with the aid of his sister Electra.

The tragic story of Agamemnon's homecoming was well known to Homer's audience, as was the happier story of the return of Odysseus, and it is thought likely that there were epic poems based on this story current in Homeric times. Homer's many allusions to the story of Agamemnon heighten the emotional intensity of his tale and the frequent comparisons of Clytemnestra with the faithful Penelope help him to enrich his characterization of the wife of Odysseus.

The story of Agamemnon was one of the most widely circulated Greek legends, partly because of the prominence given it by Homer. In later times it provided plots for many dramatic works by Aeschylus, Sophocles, Euripides, and other tragedians.

BOOK IV

TELEMACHUS AND MENELAUS

Summary

When Telemachus and Peisistratus arrive at the palace of Menelaus, they find a great feast in progress, celebrating the impending weddings of the king's son and daughter. They are welcomed warmly and after bathing and putting on fresh clothing, they are given seats of honor in the banquet hall.

Proper etiquette does not permit a guest to be questioned before he has dined, so Menelaus does not yet know who his visitors are. In the course of conversation he refers several times to his old, dear friend Odysseus and upon hearing this, Telemachus begins to weep. Queen Helen joins the group and immediately notices the resemblance between the son and the father. When she mentions this, Peisistratus identifies his companion and himself, and explains their mission. Menelaus decides that it would not be decent to discuss Telemachus' business until the morning, since so many present at the feast have sad memories of the Trojan War. He and Helen recount a few of the more brilliant exploits of Odysseus at the siege and then all retire to bed.

The next day Menelaus and Telemachus have a private meeting. Telemachus explains the situation at Ithaca and his desire for knowledge of his father. Menelaus becomes indignant upon learning of the crudity and greed of the suitors. He tells Telemachus of his adventures in Egypt after the end of the war. During the course of his travels he had encountered Proteus, the Old Man of the Sea, whom he was able to force to give him information. After he had learned how he could return safely to Sparta, he had inquired about the well-being of his former comrades. Proteus told him the names of those who had safely reached home and those who had died; he also described the murder of Agamemnon and mentioned that Odysseus was alive, but was detained on the distant island of the nymph Calypso. Telemachus thanks the king for his aid and prepares to leave, but before he goes, Menelaus gives him many valuable gifts.

Meanwhile, on Ithaca, the suitors have discovered that Telemachus has really sailed, despite their efforts to prevent the voyage. Led by Antinous and Eurymachus, they prepare a ship of their own and plot to ambush and kill the young prince in the straits leading to the island. Penelope also had been ignorant of the expedition and when Medon, her faithful herald, tells her of it she is immediately overcome by grief and worry. Her servants attempt to comfort her, but with little success, and the queen remains locked in her room, crying and refusing to eat. That night Athene sends a dream in which Penelope's sister appears to her and reassures her of the safety of Telemachus.

Commentary

Another interesting contrast with the *Iliad* appears in this and the preceding book, for a complete transformation has taken place in the values and outlooks of the heroes of the Trojan War. In the *Odyssey* they are depicted as comfort-loving, self-satisfied noblemen, whose ideals are those of courtliness and mannered living, social order and stability, material prosperity and domestic peace. All of the exaltation of chivalry, martial prowess, honor, and the achievement of personal renown is gone, not only here, but throughout the poem as is best illustrated in the statement of Achilles when Odysseus visits him later in Hades, Book XI, "...I would rather be a serf in the house of some landless man, with little enough for himself to live on, than king of all these dead men that have done with life." The fabulous Helen now seems more like a respectable middle-class matron than the kind of woman over whom two great armies would fight for ten years.

These differences are partly explained by the fact that the heroes of the *Iliad* are older now than they were at Troy and are seen at home rather than on campaign, but these considerations do not provide an adequate answer, for the Odyssean world is a more placid, less vital and less heroic place than that of the *Iliad*, and a few years of age could not cause this. Such a striking contrast in the atmosphere and underlying social background of the two poems had led some scholars to believe that the *Iliad* and the *Odyssey* are the products of different eras and social environments and could not possibly have been written by the same man.

The meetings of Telemachus with Nestor and his son in Book III and with Menelaus and Helen in this book introduce the young man to a whole new world of experience and outlook. Until now he has led an isolated and sheltered life on Ithaca, but he is beginning the journey, which in some ways parallels that of his father, which will conclude in his personal maturation and his recognition as a man by gods and mortals.

BOOK V

ODYSSEUS DEPARTS FROM CALYPSO

Summary

At the divine assembly on Olympus, Athene once more raises the question of returning Odysseus to his home. Zeus finally agrees and dispatches Hermes, his messenger, to the far-off island of Ogygia where the nymph Calypso has detained Odysseus, in the hope of making him her husband.

When he arrives, Hermes finds Odysseus sitting on a bench, yearning for his family, and weeping. The god delivers his message to Calypso who, though becoming very bitter upon hearing it, consents, since she knows she cannot defy the all-powerful Zeus. After Hermes goes back to Olympus, she tells Odysseus that she will help him return to Ithaca. The hero is at first understandably suspicious of the nymph's motives, but he is eventually reassured. With her aid, he builds himself a small boat and outfits it with all the necessary gear and provisions. When the work is completed, he eagerly sets sail for his home.

As this takes place, Poseidon returns from Ethiopia, where he had been during all these events, and sees Odysseus sailing along. His anger is aroused and raising his trident, he stirs up a savage storm. Amid the rain, wind, and waves of the tempest, the small boat of Odysseus capsizes and breaks up, and Odysseus is left in the raging sea, clinging to a bit of the wreckage, struggling to keep afloat. With the aid of Athene and the sea nymph, Leucothoie, however, he manages, despite great danger and suffering, to reach land on the island of Scheria, the home of the Phaeacians. The exhausted hero staggers ashore and takes shelter among some olive bushes, where he immediately falls asleep.

Commentary

Although our attention has been concentrated on Odysseus from the very beginning of the poem, he does not make his first appearance until this book. From this point on, however, he will be at the center of all that happens.

Odysseus is basically the same man who was seen in the *Iliad,* but his personality is given much wider expression in the *Odyssey* and he is drawn with more depth and complexity. Among the unique aspects of the characterization of Odysseus are the ways in which he differs from the typical epic hero. Odysseus combines the usual physical valor and prowess with intellect, quick wit, subtlety, and self-discipline, and is well able to live by brain as well as brawn. He is not rigid in his adherence to the heroic code of conduct (he lies, uses poisoned arrows, etc.) and adapts his behavior to the circumstances in which he finds himself, although always retaining a realistic conception of his self-interest and his ultimate goals. These are attributes which have made some critics call Odysseus the first "modern man."

Analysis of the personality of Odysseus is complicated by his possession of what seem to be two contradictory sets of motives and attitudes — sometimes he appears as a homesick, weary traveler whose only desire is to return home to his beloved wife and son; at other times he is a solitary, restless wanderer, endlessly driven by a lust for new experience and more complete knowledge (the temptation by which the Sirens try to entice him in Book XII). His complex personality is best illustrated by the epithet Homer most often uses to describe him, "Odysseus, the man of many wiles." No other character, in either Homeric epic, has a personality with so many facets and ramifications. At different times Odysseus exhibits nearly all kinds and degrees of human behavior and, without seeming inconsistent, can, depending on circumstances, be brave or cowardly, wise or foolish, cautious or foolhardy, and so on, through the whole range of human possibilities. This characteristic ambivalence of behavior and outlook, and the mystical series of adventures he undergoes, make Odysseus a symbolic figure whose life embodies the whole sum of human experience. From this point of view, the wanderings and adventures of Odysseus in the years after the fall of Troy can be interpreted as evolutionary stages in the development of humanity, or as a symbolic cleansing and maturation he must undergo before he is entitled once again to take his place in human society after the dehumanizing experience of war. From either viewpoint, his saga is an individualized version of the experiences which civilize men and make them human.

The questing aspect of the personality of Odysseus has fascinated many post-Homeric writers and because of it Odysseus is often viewed as an original faustian hero. He has been kept alive in the western literary tradition by the roles given him in many great works of literature, in all of which his legendary adventures are expanded or explained, and his personality reshaped to suit the problems of new times. The list of notable writers and poets who have adapted Odysseus to their needs is a long one, including such names as Horace, a Roman poet of the 1st Century B.C., Dante, Lord Tennyson, Ezra Pound, James Joyce, and Nikos Kazantzakis.

BOOKS VI-VIII

ODYSSEUS AMONG THE PHAEACIANS

Summary
The next morning the exhausted and starving Odysseus is discovered by Princess Nausicaa and some of her handmaidens while they are picnicking and doing the palace laundry near the river

where he was washed ashore. They feed and clothe him and direct him to the city. Odysseus goes to the palace of King Alcinous and Queen Arete, where he is received with great kindness and generosity. The royal couple promise to help him make his way to Ithaca. A day or so later, at a banquet of the Phaecian nobility, Odysseus reveals his true identity and tells the story of his adventures during the nine years after the fall of Troy.

Commentary

Odysseus' restrained and gentlemanly behavior upon meeting Nausicaa after having spent three days struggling in the sea without food or rest is a good example of his self-discipline and ability to understand and adapt quickly to the requirements of a given situation.

The land of Phaeacia where Odysseus now finds himself is a utopian, fairy-tale place where life is always easy and where all of the people are prosperous, wise, virtuous and happy. Alcinous and Arete are idealized portraits of the perfect rulers. Their kingdom is the human paradise.

The story of the sudden appearance of the stranger Odysseus in the king's palace as a helpless suppliant, his acceptance by the royal court, restoration to his true status and identity, and the hints of the love of the young maiden Nausicaa for the unknown older man, have many parallels in Celtic and oriental folklore. The tale is similar to some of the stories in the *Arabian Nights* and to parts of old ballads from Ireland and Britain. Within the framework of the *Odyssey*, the visit to Phaeacia, the paradise where all human problems are solved and all needs are fulfilled, can be interpreted as an inspired vision, granted Odysseus after his purification and transformation, of the highest and most perfect form of human life.

The delightful characterization of Nausicaa is one of Homer's most popular and has been almost universally praised by critics and readers. Samuel Butler, the Victorian author and translator of Homer, once attempted to prove that Nausicaa was the real writer of the *Odyssey*, and an intriguing novel, *Homer's Daughter* has been developed from this idea by Robert Graves.

BOOK IX

THE WANDERINGS OF ODYSSEUS – THE CICONES, THE LOTUS-EATERS, AND THE CYCLOPS

ummary

Odysseus identifies himself to the eager audience and begins is story. After leaving Troy, he and his men had made a raid on he land of the Cicones. Despite an initial success, they were ultinately defeated and escaped only after suffering numerous casualies. The ships sailed on, battling a severe storm, until they reached he country of the Lotus-Eaters. The inhabitants of this strange land vere friendly, but those of the seamen who ate of the lotus, a local lant, quickly lost all memory of home and duty. Odysseus and he men who had not been exposed to the lotus were hard-pressed o rescue those who had been affected by this narcotic.

Sailing on, farther westward, they eventually came to the is-and of the Cyclops, a wild race of one-eyed giants. Leaving most f his men in a sheltered cove, Odysseus with only one ship landed n the island and he, with a party of twelve, went ashore.

The group wandered about until they came across a huge cave, utfitted with a shepherd's equipment, and they went inside to wait the owner. After a while, a huge Cyclops named Polyphemus ame back to the cave, driving his flocks before him, and when he ad returned all the animals to their pens, he pushed a gigantic tone in front of the mouth of the cave. When Polyphemus discovered the Achaeans in his den, he immediately devoured two of hem, sarcastically promising to eat the others shortly. An appeal o the mercy of Zeus was of no avail, for the savage giant defied he power of the king of the gods. In the morning, after killing two nore of the men, he took his flocks back to the fields and locked the urvivors in the cave by replacing the vast stone at the entrance.

Odysseus and his men realized that even if they were able to ill the giant as he slept, they would achieve nothing, since they vould not be able to move the barrier at the cave mouth. However, the shrewd captain devised a plan and they sharpened and hid a long olive pole. When Polyphemus returned that evening, Odysseus plied him with wine until the Cyclops fell into a drunken sleep. Before the giant passed out, he insisted upon knowing Odysseus name. The wily Achaean answered, "Nobody."

As Polyphemus slept, Odysseus and his men stabbed him in the eye with the pole, blinding him. The giant screamed with rage and pain but could not find his assailants. His cries attracted the other Cyclops, but when he told them that "Nobody" was responsible for his wound, they assumed that one of the gods was involved and wandered off.

In the morning, the Cyclops reopened the cave so as to allow his sheep to graze. Although he tried to prevent anyone from escaping by feeling everything that passed through the entrance, Odysseus and his men got out by clinging to the bellies of the sheep.

Upon reaching their ship again, the Achaeans set sail at once in great terror. Every member of the crew rowed with the furious energy of fear. While still near the island, Odysseus foolishy shouted out to the Cyclops, bragging about his exploit. The giant frantically hurled great boulders in the direction of the sounds, but fortunately all missed the target. Odysseus was carried away in his pride and unwisely announced his identity to the pain-stricken giant. As the ship passed out of range of his stones, Polyphemus called upon his father, Poseidon, to punish the man who had harmed him.

Commentary

In this book Odysseus begins to tell about his adventures from the fall of Troy to the time he arrived on Calypso's island nine years later. Most of the adventures he has had are derived from folktales, as already mentioned, and have been adapted by Homer to suit the needs of his poem and the tastes of his audience. Although none of the adventures is historical in this strict sense, it is sometimes possible to find in the stories a reflection of historical realities in the time of Homer.

The Cicones are usually thought to be a tribe living somewhere in Thrace, a region not far from Troy, which the Achaeans would have to sail past on their way home. The Achaean seafaring chieftains are known to have been freebooters who engaged in commerce only when piracy was impossible. The raid of Odysseus and his men on the Cicone city of Ismaurus is a good example of this tendency. It is the most realistic and unsupernatural of all the adventures of Odysseus. It is generally accepted by most scholars as being a true story of the real Odysseus or, at least, a true picture of the way of life of chieftains of the Homeric period.

Some scholars believe that the land of the Lotus-Eaters was located in North Africa, but others have claimed other locations. It is also occasionally said that the story of the Lotus plant contains a distorted reference to some kind of narcotic poppy plant known to have been cultivated in North Africa in later times, but this kind of magical plant is a typical element of many fairy tales and may have no historical reference.

The story of Odysseus and Polyphemus is interesting for several reasons. Although Odysseus' motive for landing on the unknown island of the Cyclops is his over-riding intellectual curiosity, he demonstrates an unusual lack of prudence in allowing himself and his men to be captured in the cave. Moreover, his adventures after leaving the island are all of a mystical character and he seems a changed man, as symbolized by his casting off of his old identity when he says his name is "Nobody."

The episode has been explained in a symbolic sense as crystallizing an underlying main theme of the poem. In blinding Polyphemus, whose father is the sea god Poseidon, the wandering seafarer Odysseus challenged the forces of nature. This is symbolic of the way that all Greeks pitted themselves against nature when they first took to the sea, the source of life.

Odysseus' blinding of Polyphemus is also symbolic of the challenge that all men face when they attempt to harness the forces of nature to civilize the untamed world which they have inherited. The escape of Odysseus from the island, his personal transformation and rebirth, and his eventual safe return to Ithaca, show that nature can interfere with and impede human progress but that nature cannot conquer mankind so long as men are willing to face hardship and accept the consequences of their struggle.

Homer's description of the blind Polyphemus with his favorite ram at the door of the cave illustrates the poet's great compassion and is one of the most famous passages in the *Odyssey*.

BOOK X

THE WANDERINGS OF ODYSSEUS – AEOLUS, THE LAESTRYGONIANS, AND CIRCE

Summary

After a few more days of sailing, Odysseus and his men landed on the island of Aeolus, the king of the winds. The Achaean seafarers were greeted warmly and entertained in the royal palace. Upon their departure, Aeolus gave Odysseus a gift: a large leather bag which contained all the adverse winds which could drive his ships off course. They set sail again and in ten days were within sight of Ithaca.

While Odysseus slept, his crew began muttering and dissension quickly spread through the ship. The jealous men assumed that the bag from Aeolus contained valuable treasures and were resentful that their captain had not shared with them. Finally curiosity overwhelmed them and they ripped open the bag, setting all the winds free. A great gale arose at once and the ships were blown far from Ithaca, back to Aeolia. Although Odysseus asked for forgiveness and help, Aeolus refused and cursing him as a sinner and enemy of the gods, banished the hero from his island. The wanderers were forced to set sail again without the benefit of any wind at all, so the crews had to strain at their oars. Several days later the ships landed on the island of the Laestrygonians. These vicious cannibals attacked the unsuspecting sailors, and all the ships, except that of Odysseus, were sunk. The survivors, mourning their dead comrades, sailed on until they reached the island of Aeaea, the home of the goddess Circe.

After camping on the beach for a few days, Odysseus sent half his men under the command of Eurylochus to explore this seemingly uninhabited island. Shortly afterward this officer returned alone, telling a strange tale. The men had been lured into a lavish villa in the center of the isle by a strange and beautiful woman. After she had fed and entertained them, she had waved a wand and they had all been transformed into swine. She and her servants had locked them in a pen where they were now wallowing in the mud and grime. He alone had stayed outside the palace, because of his suspicious nature, and so had escaped.

This weird story terrified the remaining men, but Odysseus was resolute and set out alone to rescue the victims. On the way he encountered Hermes, in the guise of a young nobleman, and this god instructed him on how to behave with the enchantress. He also gave Odysseus a wondrous magic herb called Moly with which to protect himself.

On his arrival, Circe received Odysseus graciously and then attempted to bewitch him, but all her spells were of no avail. He soon overcame her and when he threatened her life, she returned his men to human form. After these events, Circe recognized Odysseus as someone whose eventual arrival on her island had been predicted and whose acquaintance she had eagerly anticipated. The two soon became lovers and he and his crew stayed at her home for nearly a year.

When this time had elapsed, the Achaeans again began to yearn for Ithaca. Odysseus held Circe to an old promise to help him return home and she agreed. However, she pointed out to him, in order to have a safe voyage he must go to Hades, the land of the dead, to consult the spirit of the prophet Tiresias. She gave him full directions for his journey to the end of the world and provided him with provisions and the necessary animals for sacrifice. And so, Odysseus and his travel-worn men set sail once more.

Commentary

After the great victory over Polyphemus, a portent of the coming triumph over Poseidon and nature, a reminder is necessary that human power is limited; that the forces of nature, while they can be turned to human use and profit, can never be completely subjugated. The re-education of Odysseus demonstrates man's capacity to control his environment, but in the episode of the bag of winds given by Aeolus, the human weaknesses, symbolized by the crew of Odysseus, which always make man's relation with nature tenuous and uncertain come into play. The lesson is that maturity and discipline are required and that natural forces are not toys, but dangerous, though helpful, tools.

The Laestrygonians are cannibals. They may be purely fictional creations, but some scholars believe that this episode is based on tales of the experiences of Greek seafarers in faraway regions of the Mediterranean basin or the Black Sea, or even along the coast of West Africa, where Phoenecian ships are known to have sailed in somewhat later times.

The encounter of Odysseus with the witch Circe is based on a motif common in European folklore, though several changes have been made in the conventional pattern of the story (for example, the replacement by Hermes of what would once have been a benevolent forest spirit or a mysterious, bearded old man; the location of the story on an island rather than deep in an inland forest; and the fact that Odysseus never uses the magical Moly plant after having received it from Hermes). A familiar variant of the same folktale, though in a much changed and much more recent form, is "Hansel and Gretel," first recorded by the Grimm Brothers in the 19th century.

BOOK XI

THE WANDERINGS OF ODYSSEUS – THE DESCENT INTO HADES

Summary

Following the instructions given by Circe, Odysseus sailed to the very edge of the world. Here he and his men made libations of milk, honey, wine, and water to the dead. Then Odysseus offered

prayers and sacrified a ram and a black ewe, pouring their blood
into a trench. At once hordes of dead souls began to rush out of
Hades attracted by the odor of the fresh blood. Odysseus held off
the throng with his sword, awaiting Tiresias.

The blind sear finally arrived and after drinking some of the
blood, advised Odysseus about his return home. He warned the
hero of the various dangers that still awaited him on his journey
and how he would finally arrive at Ithaca unknown and friendless.
After further difficulties, he would re-establish himself as master of
his house, but his wanderings would not end until he was able to regain the favor of Poseidon. Achieving this, Odysseus would live
out a long and peaceful life.

When Tiresias had departed, Odysseus conversed with many
other dead souls, all of whom were eager for news of their friends
and loved ones who still lived. Those to whom he spoke included
Anticleia, his mother, who had died after he left for Troy, Agamemnon, Achilles, and Elpenor, a member of his crew who had
died on Circe's island. He also met Tantalus, Sisyphus, Heracles,
Phaeadra, Ariadne, Jocasta, and other great men and women of the
past. Finally the sight of so many of the dead grew unbearable
and Odysseus fled to his ship. With sighs of relief, his men made
for the open sea again.

Commentary

The visit of Odysseus to Hades embodies another common
folkloric motif and has many parallels even in Greek mythology, for
example in the legends about Orpheus, Theseus, and Hercules. This
episode serves several important functions in the context of the
story by providing an opportunity for more contrasts with the fate
of Agamemnon, by giving a new view of the Trojan War and the
heroic ideal which Odysseus is superseding during his wanderings
through the conversation with Achilles; and by demonstrating the
consequences of the long absence of Odysseus from Ithaca through
his unexpected meeting with his dead mother.

The encounters of Odysseus with so many important and
evocative figures from the whole Greek legendary tradition during

his visit to the afterworld, serves to heighten his perception and broadens his intellectual frame of reference to include all that is important in the common experience of his people. Thus, this episode can be regarded as the decisive step in his re-education and, at the same time, as a symbolic death and rebirth which he must undergo to prepare for his return home where, in a sense, he will take up a new life. The motif of death and rebirth is also a common one in Mediterranean mythology. It plays an important part in many mythical stories about gods and semi-divine heroes, among whom are Adonis and Osiris.

BOOK XII

THE WANDERINGS OF ODYSSEUS – THE SIRENS, SCYLLA AND CHARYBDIS, AND THE CATTLE OF THE SUN

Summary

Odysseus and his men returned to Aeaea to bury Elpenor, in fulfilment of the poor sailor's last request. Circe again provided them with the supplies for their journey and gave Odysseus further detailed instructions about the hazards of the next leg of the voyage. Its crew confident and in high spirits, the ship set sail once more.

First the island of the Sirens had to be passed. These irresistible women attracted unwary mariners with their beautiful songs and lured them onto the reefs surrounding their island, where many ships already had been wrecked. Odysseus plugged the ears of his crew with wax so that they were immune to the tantalizing music. Since he wished to hear the song, however, he had himself lashed to the mast. When the voices of the Sirens became audible he unsuccessfully strained to free himself, but as he struggled, the ship passed this danger unharmed.

They then came upon the twofold horror of Scylla and Charybdis. Scylla was a ferocious monster with six heads who sat upon a cliff and devoured passing seamen. Across a narrow strait was Charybdis, a fierce whirlpool. To pass between both unscathed was impossible. The ship was safely steered around the whirlpool, but though Odysseus attempted to fight, six terror-striken members of his crew were lost to Scylla.

Shortly after this costly and perilous passage, the ship landed on the island where Hyperion, the sun god, kept his cattle and was becalmed there for a month. Despite the warnings of Tiresias and Circe, Odysseus was unable to control his men. Led by Eurylochus they slaughtered some of the divine cattle for a meal, thereby incurring the wrath of all the gods. When they sailed from the island, a storm came up and one of the thunderbolts of Zeus destroyed the ship, killing the entire crew. Odysseus was thrown overboard and narrowly escaped being drowned in Charybdis, as he was driven back through the strait. After nine more days of aimless drifting in the raging sea, he was washed ashore on Ogygia, the home of Calypso. Here Odysseus ends his story to the Phaeacians since he has already told of his seven years stay with the nymph and his eventual escape from her clutches.

Commentary

The Sirens, who represent one of the most dangerous temptations the newly born Odysseus must face, try to lure him by appealing to that aspect of his personality which has always made him different from his friends and colleagues — his intellectual curiosity and zest for knowledge — but having learned the value of prudence from his experience with Polyphemus, Odysseus cautiously protects himself and his men and safely passes the obstacle. It is possible to view this encounter with the Sirens as the first of a series of tests which he must now pass to demonstrate that he is worthy of the rebirth he has gone through and the exalted vision he will be granted when he arrives at the land of the Phaeacians. The safe passage beyond the rocks where the Sirens live shows that Odysseus has been transformed by his experiences. He knows now that the scope of human attainment is limited and has accepted this, in a way that Achilles, for example, was never able to do. His crew, on the other hand, have not learned this lesson, as was shown when they inadvertently released the winds given Odysseus by Aeolus and thus overreached themselves to the point of great danger. This failure to perceive the proper sphere and dimension of human activity is the cause of their deaths on the island of the Sun.

It has been suggested by some scholars that Scylla and Charybdis are a distorted reference to the dangers of the Straits of Messina in the forbidding and (to Homeric Greeks) unknown western Mediterranean. Others have said they represent a whirlpool and an octopus. Regardless of which claim is correct, this incident can also be interpreted as another test which Odysseus must undergo, a temporal test as opposed to the spiritual test of the Sirens.

Most of the stories in the four preceding books are imaginary adventures which are much older than Homer and cannot, as already pointed out, be regarded as historical, even when localized in some specific geographical area. Within the framework of the poem, it is possible to give them a symbolic meaning which enriches the story of Odysseus, but many interpretations are possible and there is no way of knowing whether Homer ever intended such meanings to be read into his poem.

With this warning kept in mind, it may be interesting to see in what other ways the *Odyssey* has been interpreted. One folklorist school of thought claims that the adventures of Odysseus are really rationalized and expurgated accounts of ancient religious rituals which were no longer understood even in the time of Homer and which date back to the earliest times. In his book *The Hero*, for example, the English folklorist Lord Raglan explains the Wanderings of Odysseus as a confused account of the ritual tour of his domain that would have been made by a divine solar king of the kind that reigned in the Mediterranean area centuries before the Indo-European tribes ever settled in Greece. According to Raglan, all the incidents mentioned by Odysseus in his account of his wandering contain elements of ancient religious practice — the blinding of Polyphemus, for instance, being a reinactment of the ritual kindling of the sacred fire at the beginning of a new reign.

Another group interprets the Wanderings in psychological terms. Professor Joseph Campbell, in his book *The Masks of God: Occidental Mythology*, writes that Odysseus is a hero whose adventures reinact a primitive solar mythology which was itself an intellectual response to emotional needs that are today expressed in much different form, what he calls "psychological adventures in the mythic realm of the archetypes of the soul," that is to say, that the symbols of such ancient mythology as the Odysseus story are spontaneous expressions of psychological truths and needs akin to those rediscovered by psychologists of the Jungian group.

There are still other groups of scholars who eschew symbolic interpretation altogether and claim that the Wanderings are nothing more than distorted historical memories, and who have tried to explain them in more precise historical terms and to localize them in various regions of the Mediterranean basin, ranging from the far west and North Africa to the Black Sea coast and the Levant.

It is worth noting that none of these different ways of interpreting the Odysseus story contradicts the others, since they all approach it on different levels and for different purposes, so that it is possible to harmonize them into one comprehensive system if one wishes. But, whatever the real meaning and origin of the legendary tales in the *Odyssey*, there is no doubt that these were forgotten many years before the time of Homer, and it is important to remember that we find these tales integrated into a romantic adventure story in which their only purpose is to entertain. Analysis of the stories in mythological, psychological, philosophical, or historical terms may be edifying and valuable, but it is in no way necessary for appreciation of the *Odyssey* as a complete-in-itself work of art and literature.

BOOKS XIII-XVI

ODYSSEUS RETURNS TO ITHACA

Summary

The generous Phaeacians give Odysseus many valuable gifts and transport him to Ithaca in one of their magic ships. They are punished afterward by Poseidon for their kindness to his enemy. Meanhile, Odysseus is met on the beach by Athene. She disguises him as an old beggar so he can learn the situation on the island and make his plans without being recognized.

After leaving Athene, Odysseus goes into the hills to the farm of Eumaeus the swineherd, one of his few loyal servants, where he is welcomed and treated kindly despite his disguise. Shortly afterward Telemachus returns to Ithaca from Sparta and also goes to the farm. While Eumaeus is away on an errand, Odysseus reveals his identity to his son and they begin to lay their plans. The return of Odysseus will be kept secret even from Penelope and Laertes. Telemachus will go back to the palace as if nothing had happened. Odysseus will follow, still in disguise. At the opportune moment, they will take vengeance on the suitors.

Commentary

After the great build-up of tension and the swift movement of the action in the books treating the wanderings and adventures of Odysseus, these books seem much more relaxed. The pace of the story has slowed down to make more believable the transition from the fabulous world of the supernatural in which Odysseus has spent the last ten years and the real world on Ithaca where he hopes to regain the kingship and again take up his old life.

The meeting of Odysseus with Eumaeus is important because it gives the reader a chance to see and judge Odysseus through the eyes of someone who is neither his friend nor his relative. The swineherd's description of his master reinforces the favorable impression of Odysseus that has already been created and develops previously unknown facets of his personality, such as his kind conduct toward social inferiors.

The journey of Telemachus to Sparta and Pylos has done nothing to locate Odysseus and has in no way assisted the development of the plot, but the youth's experiences in the great outer world have matured him. He has a new sense of self-confidence and personal dignity. In every sense of the word, Telemachus has now become a man, worthy of his heroic father and of the patronage of Athene, and capable of taking his place at the side of Odysseus in the coming struggle against the suitors.

BOOK XVII

ODYSSEUS GOES INTO THE TOWN

Summary

In the morning, Telemachus returns to the town and calls upon his mother. Penelope is overjoyed to have her son at home again. She listens eagerly to his report of his hospitable welcome by Nestor and Menelaus and of the rumor that Odysseus might still be alive on the island of the nymph Calypso. Telemachus introduces his mother to the fugitive Theoclymenus and this man, who claims to be a soothsayer, asserts that Odysseus, in disguise, is already somewhere on Ithaca and will soon avenge himself on the suitors. Penelope does not believe this tale, although she would like to very much.

Shortly afterward, Eumaeus and Odysseus also set out for the palace. On the way they encounter Melanthius, the chief goatherd. This wicked servant of the royal house is disloyal and an appeaser of the suitors. When he sees the old beggar, he insults him cruelly and, without provocation, kicks him. Odysseus' hot temper is aroused, but he has a role to play and is able to control himself. He is defended from further harm by Eumaeus.

At the gateway of the palace, the two men discover an old and toothless dog lying uncared for in a pile of filth. Eumaeus explains that this is Argus, once the favorite hound of Odysseus, who is now sick and near death. His master has been gone for nineteen years and everyone ignores the helpless animal. At the sight of Odysseus, the old dog lifts his head and whimpers, then dies. A tear trickles down Odysseus' check, unseen by Eumaeus.

The two enter the palace, where the suitors are at their banquet tables. Telemachus provides Odysseus with a place to sit and some food, and gives him permission to beg from the guests. All give him something except Antinous, their leader, who reviles Odysseus and hits him with a footstool. Odysseus curses Antinous and even some of the suitors are aroused by this needless sadism. Odysseus and Telemachus both silently swear their revenge for this act.

Penelope asks Eumaeus about the stranger and then suggests that he be brought to her in order to tell his story and to offer any news he may have of her husband. Odysseus agrees to see her that night.

Commentary

From here until Book XXII there will be a gradual and dramatic increase in tension as the doom of the suitors is predicted and foreshadowed in many different ways, and as their own behavior seals their fate. The entangling web of their sins will become more and more tight until it is impossible for them to escape the retribution which the gods have ordained and they have earned, for they will ignore all warnings and every opportunity given them for reformation or repentance. The rumor that Odysseus is still alive told Telemachus by Nestor and Menelaus and repeated by him to Penelope, and the prophecy of Theoclymenus, are the first of many events that progressively deepen the ominous atmosphere. The suitors' mistreatment of Odysseus, still disguised as a beggar, and the cruelty of the disloyal servant Melanthius, also contribute to this dark mood, by showing that the suitors and their collaborators are completely sinful, not only because they have badgered Penelope but also because they maltreat the innocent and helpless, and thus that they are entitled to no clemency whatsoever.

The scene of the death of the faithful old hunting dog Argus is one of the most moving in the *Odyssey*. It has been praised for its beautiful sentiment, its perceptive understanding of animals, and the brilliant descriptive realism with which it is narrated.

BOOK XVIII

THE FIGHT BETWEEN ODYSSEUS AND IRUS; THE SUITORS TORMENT ODYSSEUS

Summary

That afternoon, as the suitors exercise themselves in the court-yard, Irus, another beggar whom many of them are fond of, arrives at the palace. This vagabond is a big, portly man and quite a braggart. He immediately begins to bully Odysseus, to the amusement of the onlookers. He threatens to thrash the old man unless he leaves Ithaca at once, for, says Irus, Ithaca is his private province for begging and he tolerates no competition. Odysseus retorts angrily and the suitors, led by Antinous, arrange a boxing match between the two vagrants, with mock awards for the victor. Irus struts about, playing the hero and boasting about how he will win, but when the combatants undress, everyone is amazed at the muscular body possessed by Odysseus. The cowardly Irus attempts to avoid the fight, but Antinous will not allow this and though Odysseus tries to pull his punches, he breaks the bully's jaw. The suitors congratulate Odysseus and give him his prizes and then return to the hall for dinner. Odysseus tries to warn Amphinomous, the kindest of them of the impending danger to the suitors, but the young man pays hir no heed.

Penelope makes an appearance before the suitors, after cai fully grooming herself, and with her beauty enhanced by Athene. The lovely queen evokes the admiration of all who see her. She expresses her indignation at the fight which has just taken place and then chides the suitors for continuing to exhaust the resources of her husband's estate. The noblemen are shamed by this and send their servants to bring gifts for the queen from their homes or ships.

At dinner that evening Odysseus rebukes Melantho, one of the maidservants of the household, who has become the mistress of Eurymachus, for her lack of loyalty. His jibes drive her and the other serving girls from the hall. He and Eurymachus engage in an argument and the young man throws a stool at Odysseus. Odysseus ducks and one of the stewards is hit. Everyone present grows excited and in the uproar Telemachus suggests that they all go home for the night in order to calm down. Despite their surprise at Telemachus' audacity, the suitors do so.

Commentary

The fight between Odysseus and Irus is a humorous diversion which also serves to illustrate from another direction the insolence and sinfulness of the suitors, for they are concerned only with their own amusement and care nothing about the suffering or feelings of other people. At the same time, the unexpected victory of Odysseus over the "champion" they have selected to represent them symbolizes their inner corruption and his inner strength, and is a portent of their ultimate downfall and his triumph.

BOOK XIX

PENELOPE MEETS ODYSSEUS DISGUISED AS A BEGGAR; EURYCLEIA RECOGNIZES ODYSSEUS

Summary

After the suitors have left, Odysseus and Telemachus clear the hall and remove all the weapons that are stored there. They hide the arms in another part of the palace under lock and key. When they have completed this task, Odysseus sends Telemachus off to bed. Penelope and her maids now come down to the hall in order to clean it. Melantho and Odysseus again quarrel, but the queen severely scolds the insolent girl.

As the servants work, Penelope and Odysseus converse. She tells him about the long absence of her husband and of the continued ordeal she has faced in dealing with the suitors. The queen explains how she has tried to put the suitors off by every means at her disposal, including tricks, lies, and excuses about her son being too young for her to remarry. Now, however, Telemachus is a grown man and she will soon be forced to make a choice. Odysseus is deeply touched by this story and has to strive hard with himself in order to remain silent. Penelope then asks Odysseus about himself and the wily hero invents a tale, involving many hardships, in which he claims to have been acquainted with her husband. The authentic information about Odysseus which he provides moves the queen, as does the beggar's statement that Odysseus is still alive and on his way home. Penelope must supervise her servants at their work, but before she leaves she asks one of her maids to bathe the old man's tired and worn feet.

Eurycleia, the aged nurse of Odysseus, is assigned this task. As she washes him, she suddenly recognizes an old scar on his leg and realizes that this is her master. She is about to tell the queen when Odysseus sternly warns her that his identity, for the time being, must be kept a strict secret from everyone. The old woman agrees to remain silent.

Penelope returns to Odysseus and tells him that she has decided on a method to satisfy the suitors and select one of them. There will be a contest in which they will be asked to duplicate one of her husband's most famous feats. Using Odysseus' bow, they will be required to shoot an arrow through a straight row of twelve axes. The winner will become her new husband. The beggar agrees that this is a good idea and predicts that Odysseus will return home before any of the suitors is able to string his bow, but Penelope does not understand the import of his remark. While Odysseus prepares a bed for himself on the floor of the deserted hall, Penelope returns to her room. There she is overcome by the memory of her lost husband and weeps into the night, until Athene helps her to fall asleep.

Commentary

Now that Odysseus is back on Ithaca and has been admitted to the palace, the pace of the story begins to quicken. Penelope finally announces her readiness to marry one of the suitors. This sudden change in her attitude after ten years of fidelity expresses her sad conviction that Odysseus is dead after all, but it also introduces a new source of tension—the question whether or not Odysseus has returned home in time, whether he will be able to prevent the marriage, and whether Penelope will accept him after having decided to select another husband. Moreover, during their conversation together, Penelope several times nearly recognizes Odysseus and the old nurse does, but is silenced before she blurts out his name. This kind of building of suspense is unusual in Greek saga poetry and may be due to changes introduced by Homer into the original conclusion of the legend of the hero's return which he was using in his poem. Comparison with other folkloric literature indicates that in the original the wife may actually have recognized the husband through his disguise because of the scar and may even have been forced into accepting a new husband before his return.

BOOK XX

ODYSSEUS LAYS HIS PLANS; THE SUITORS IGNORE THEIR FINAL WARNING

Summary

During the night Odysseus tosses and turns, worrying about the coming encounter with the suitors and whether he will be victorious. Athene appears to him, however, and promises that he will have her aid in the struggle, and that this is obviously a guarantee of success. Penelope also is unable to sleep and prays to Artemis, begging that she be rescued from marriage to another man, even if it means her death.

In the morning Odysseus appeals to Zeus for a sign of his favor and is answered by the ominous rumbling of the great god's thunder. The omen is noticed by many others also and a general mood of foreboding sets in. Odysseus continues to observe the behavior of his servants in order to learn who has remained faithful. Melanthius arrives with goats for the day's banquet and persists in baiting Odysseus. Eumaeus comes to the palace also, driving hogs for slaughter and again demonstrates his goodness, and another loyal servant arrives, in the person of Philoetius, the chief cowherd, who had been on the mainland with his cattle.

The suitors, who had been again planning the assassination of Telemachus, eventually return to the palace too. As they lunch, one of their number, Ctesippus, insults Odysseus and hurls a bone at him. Telemachus is outraged by this and delivers a long tirade to the suitors in which he enumerates all their vices and misdeeds. The group is shocked by this unexpected boldness, but the minds of the suitors are befuddled by drink and they merely laugh at his warnings. The soothsayer Theoclymenus cautions them that a catastrophe is impending in which they will all be punished for their evil ways, but they are beyond reforming and mock the poor man until he leaves the palace in a rage. The suitors continue to drink and have a good time, but meanwhile Telemachus stays alert, waiting for his father's signal.

Commentary

During the final few hours before the culminating events of Book XXII, there are many ominous portents and there arises a general feeling of uneasiness throughout Ithaca. As the day passes, the characters engage in their usual activities mechanically and by rote, rather as if they were participants in some kind of sacred symbolic drama where every role is preordained and nothing can be altered or omitted. There is a dream-like quality to all that happens. The promise of divine sanction and support for Odysseus in the impending conflict is sealed by the rumbling of thunder sent by Zeus and by the visit of Athene to her favorite during the night, and this gives a divine aura to what might otherwise prove to be a barbaric bloodbath. Even the suitors seem to sense the approaching doom, but they are powerless to prevent or escape it, and their only re-action can be the uncomprehending confusion and panic they experience near the end of the book. The indignity to which Odysseus is made to submit at lunch by Ctesippus, the long catalogue of the suitors' misdeeds voiced by Telemachus, and the final prophecy of Theoclymenus are a last summation and explanation of the reasons for the revenge that will soon be taken: a justification in the eyes of gods and men for the killings and the purification of the house of Odysseus (symbolized later by its fumigation with burning sulphur) which parallels his personal purification during the ten years of wandering. For the new Odysseus to live in accordance with what he has learned and become during his adventures, it is necessary for outer things to be purged also so they can be harmonized with inner things.

BOOK XXI

THE CONTEST TO STRING THE BOW OF ODYSSEUS

Summary

Penelope brings the great bow of Odysseus into the hall and announces the contest to the suitors. He among them who is able to string the bow and shoot an arrow through the twelve axes will become her husband. The suitors accept the challenge, although

Antinous takes this opportunity to deride the faithful swineherd and cowherd, who are visibly upset by the reminder that their master is dead. Telemachus digs a trench and aligns the twelve axes. He then attempts to string the bow, eager to see if he is yet as strong as his father, and makes four tries. He would probably succeed on the last attempt, but Odysseus prevents him from completing it. During an interval, while the suitors prepare themselves, Odysseus takes Eumaeus and Philoetius aside and quietly identifies himself to them. The two are overcome by emotion and quickly agree to carry out the orders he gives them.

The suitors each now have an opportunity, but however they strain and despite their attempts to soften the wood by greasing and heating it, not one of them is man enough to bend the mighty bow. Finally, Antinous suggests that they postpone further efforts until the next day and this is agreed to. At this point, Odysseus, who has been sitting alone in a corner of the hall, asks for a chance to try the bow. The suitors are indignant at his request and refuse him. Penelope, however, is willing, although she assures the group that if he wins she would not marry him. Telemachus orders his mother and her women to leave the hall and then sends the bow to Odysseus. Meanwhile, unseen by the suitors, Eumaeus and Philoetius lock the gates of the palace and the doors of the hall.

Odysseus takes the bow in his hands, pretending not to hear the abuse of the suitors. Effortlessly he strings the mighty weapon and expertly fits a bronze headed arrow to it. Slowly and seemingly without concentration, he lets fly the arrow and it swiftly shoots through the row of axes. As the suitors sit stupefied by disbelief, Telemachus takes hold of his sword and spear and steps to his father's side.

Commentary

Many motifs turn up in the conclusion of the tale of the Return and Vengeance of Odysseus which illustrate the antiquity of the legend and its roots in folkloric tradition. Among these motifs are the bow of Odysseus, the marvelous weapon which is the possession of the hero and which only he can wield; the extraordinary strength and ability of the hero; and the contest in which the hero defeats many rivals to establish his right to win the bride (though in this version she is already his wife). It has also been pointed out that the appearance of Odysseus at the court of Ithaca disguised as a beggar, his restoration to his real status through victory in a contest, and the eventual recognition of his true identify are all variants of the same legendary theme which lies behind the story of his visit to the land of the Phaeacians in Books VI, VII, and VIII.

Homer's long description of how Odysseus turns the bow over in his hands and examines it closely before using it is an adroit narrative touch which heightens the tension at the decisive moment of the story's denouement. At the same time, it is a perceptive portrayal of the joyous disbelief that Odysseus feels, knowing that he is finally home and is about to establish himself in his rightful place. Another interesting touch is Homer's comment that Telemachus would have succeeded in bending the bow had he tried once more. This establishes the legitimacy of Telemachus' claim to be the son of Odysseus and is a sign that someday he will rise to be the equal of his hero father.

BOOK XXII

ODYSSEUS KILLS THE SUITORS

Summary

With a shout, Odysseus leaps to the threshhold of the hall and kills Antinous with his next arrow. The suitors are outraged and horrified by this act, and think that the old beggar has gone beserk. As they mill about in confusion, Odysseus announces who he is. Eurymachus tries to place the blame for their misdeeds on the dead Antinous and hopefully offers to make restitution for the goods they have consumed. Odysseus, however, has vowed to punish these criminals, and with his next arrow he kills Eurymachus. The suitors attempt to defend themselves with their swords, using tables and stools as shields, but they are unable to get close enough to Odysseus to do him harm. Meanwhile he continues shooting into their midst, and each arrow eliminates another enemy.

Telemachus brings our armor and spears for his father and the two loyal servants, and when the arrows are exhausted these four stand side by side and continue the battle. Several of the suitors are armed by Melanthius, who steals the weapons from the storeroom, but Eumaeus and Philoetius capture and bind him. As the fight goes on, the four comrades fight bravely and eventually all the suitors are slaughtered. Odysseus spares only Phemius the bard and Medon the herald.

The king then calls for old Eurycleia. When she sees all the bodies she prepares to sing a hymn of triumph, but Odysseus reminds her that it is impious to rejoice over the dead. He has her identify those of the maidservants who were disloyal in his absence. These twelve women are brought to the hall as prisoners. When they arrive, Odysseus forces them to remove the corpses and scrub the entire area where the battle took place. After this the women are taken outside and hanged. The treacherous Melanthius is also executed and his body is horribly mutilated. Then the scene of the battle is fumigated with sulphur and Odysseus is welcomed by those of his servants who remained faithful. He remembers all of them, despite his long absence, and breaks into tears when he is embraced by them.

Commentary

The skillful use of detail in the long account of the slaying of Antinous, the leader of the suitors, increases the vividness of this part of the story. As in other parts of the poem, Antinous is here used as a representative of the entire group.

The story of the vengeance taken by Odysseus on the suitors illustrates certain features of political and social organization in Homeric times. During that period royal power had no basis in established law or constitution and was really limited to the personal power of the man who happened to be king. The field of the Homeric king was limited primarily to war and foreign affairs, but in domestic matters issues were personal and had to be settled on a personal basis, for kings as well as commoners. Moreover, there was no form of public justice to adjudicate disputes between individuals, as a result of which there were often blood feuds to avenge murders, as is shown in Book XXIV, where the families of the dead suitors come after Odysseus. Thus, Odysseus cannot call the citizens of Ithaca to aid him in his fight to regain the throne and can depend only on himself, his family, and his loyal personal retainers.

The characteristic self-control, caution, and farsightedness which mark the personality of Odysseus all come into play in this book and the events leading up to it, for it is not likely that any other Homeric saga hero would have had the patience, discipline, or prudence so carefully to size up the situation on Ithaca, feel out the loyalties of family and servants, get acquainted with the suitors, and make a comprehensive plan before trying to take revenge. In all probability, an Achilles or a Diomedes would have immediately announced himself and taken to arms, thus running a great risk of being defeated and killed in the effort, and this kind of lack of caution is, in fact, what resulted in the death of Agamemnon. At the same time, the striking success of Odysseus in a fight against vastly superior numbers shows again that he has all the prowess and courage traditionally attributed to saga heroes and is in no way less capable than the other great chieftains who fought at Troy. Moreover, the help given him by Athene does not detract from his glory, but, rather, adds to it, for it is symbolic of the qualities of mind which enabled him to triumph against such odds.

Because of his chastening experiences over the past ten years, Odysseus, unlike other Greek saga heroes, understands the value and sanctity of human life and does not consider killing a light thing. While able to kill when necessary, he still retains a sense of the mystery of life and the presumption of taking justice or the divine right of life and death into his own hands. Thus, when Eurycleia, expresses her joy at the sight of all the dead bodies and prepares to sing a triumphal paean, Odysseus tells her, "Restrain yourself . . . and gloat in silence. I'll have no jubilation here. It is an impious thing to exult over the slain. . . ." Also, after the battle, as another recognition of the sinfulness of taking life, Odysseus orders that his house be purified by fumigation with burning sulphur. This act also reflects the purging of the grosser elements of his soul during his long journey and symbolizes his application of his new knowledge and understanding to the world in which he now expects to live. He purifies it as he has been purified.

BOOK XXIII

ODYSSEUS AND PENELOPE ARE REUNITED

Summary

Eurycleia runs upstairs eagerly and awakens her mistress, who had been put to sleep by Athene, to inform her of Odysseus' return and his bloody retribution. Penelope does not believe the story, but goes to the banquet hall to see for herself what has actually happened. Odysseus is there, but is still dressed in rags, and he is so covered with blood and filth that Penelope does not recognize him. Telemachus chides his mother for this, but Odysseus sends him away, so that the two may converse privately. When the prince is gone, Odysseus mentions certain secrets which only he and Penelope know. His wife suddenly realizes that this is, indeed, the husband for whom she had waited twenty long years, and the two greet each other tenderly.

Odysseus bathes and dresses himself in his royal garments. After arranging for the servants to keep up a pretense of dancing and feasting, to allay the suspicions of any passers-by, he and Penelope go off together to their room. The newly united couple spend the first night after their long separation making love and telling each other of the many adventures which have befallen them. The sunrise is delayed by Athene in order to give them more time alone.

In the morning, Odysseus arms himself and accompanied by Telemachus, Eumaeus, and Philoetis sets out for his father's farm.

Commentary

Some Greek critics in Hellenistic times viewed the reunion of Odysseus and Penelope in this book as the logical conclusion to the *Odyssey* and claimed that everything that follows in Book XXIV is an appendix added to Homer's original poem by some ancient interpolator. A few modern critics have agreed with this view. It will be discussed more fully after Book XXIV.

The long-expected recognition scene of Odysseus and Penelope
has been delayed until this book, where the victory over the suitors
gives it more dramatic effect. Penelope's obstinate inability to
recognize her husband after his twenty year absence, despite his
success at bending the bow, his triumph, and his acceptance by the
whole household, has been taken by some critics as an expression
of ironic humor by Homer. It can also be viewed as an emotional
over-reaction to the role she has been forced to play for so long and
to her real eagernesss to believe that the man standing before her is
her missing husband. The double standard of morality accepted in
Homeric times is shown by the unembarassed recital of Odysseus
to Penelope of all his adventures over the past years, including his
interludes with Calypso and Circe. All in all, the reunion is a happy
one, although two notes of pessimism are introduced by the reference of Odysseus to the prophecy of Tiresias given in Hades and
the precautions he has ordered to keep the slaying of the suitors
secret from the people of Ithaca.

BOOK XXIV

ODYSSEUS VISITS HIS FATHER; THE CIVIL WAR ON ITHACA IS ENDED BY THE GODS

Summary

In Hades, the shades of Achilles, Patroclus, Antilochus, Ajax,
and Agamemnon are speaking with each other when Hermes arrives, leading the souls of the dead suitors. The heroes are surprised
by this sudden influx of more than one hundred young men, and
Agamemnon inquires about the circumstances of their deaths. The
whole story is told by Amphimedon. Agamemnon is greatly im-
pressed by the prowess of Odysseus and the fidelity of his wife.

On Ithaca, Odysseus arrives at his father's house and identifies
himself to old Laertes. The joy with which the aged man greets his
son is touching. While this takes place, the Ithacans learn of the
slaughter at the palace and claim the bodies. A meeting of the Assembly is called, and though Medon and Halisthernes advocate
peace, a number of the citizens, led by Eupeithes, the father of

Antinous, decide to avenge the deaths of their sons. This group rashly arms itself and sets off for the farm of Laertes.

On Olympus, Athene consults with Zeus. The king of the gods agrees that the revenge taken by Odysseus is justified and that now peace should be restored to Ithaca. He gives his daughter a free hand to achieve this.

When the angry kinsmen of the suitors arrive at the farm, Odysseus leads out this small party to meet them. Eupeithes is killed by a spear cast by Laertes and many others are slain by Odysseus, Telemachus and the others. The attackers are fleeing in panic when Athene intervenes and orders that the conflict be brought to a conclusion. A thunderbolt of Zeus' reinforces the sanctity of this command and the battle ends Later, Athene, disguised as Mentor, establishes peace between the factions and Odysseus continues to reign as king.

Commentary

Although, as already mentioned, this book has occasionally been viewed as an appendix to the original poem, most scholars do not support this theory. They point out that Book XXIV has three main elements, all of which are quite logical and necessary in terms of the story and bring it to its natural conclusion. These are: (1) the assembly of the dead spirits, which is the natural ending to the many parallels with the story of Agamemnon, (2) the visit to Laertes, which is an obvious duty Odysseus must fulfil before the story can end, and (3) the fight with the families of the suitors, which is an inevitable result of the vengeance taken by Odysseus and a matter which must be settled (by the gods, as it turns out) lest Ithaca be torn by the strife of a blood feud and Odysseus be unable to lead a peaceful and secure life again.

As in the *Iliad,* Homer's style in the *Odyssey* has three main characteristics — complete objectivity, extreme realism, and the avoidance of romanticism. All these are aspects of the austere classicism of which he is the prime exemplar. Another Homeric characteristic which is especially evident in the *Odyssey* is his compassion and sense of the innate dignity of all life. Homer is capable of evoking pity even for the most cruel and worthless of beings, such as Polyphemus and Elpenor, and for helpless animals like Argus. Homer loved all human beings regardless of their foibles and gave stature to every character whom he depicted. Yet, though his regard for humanity is always obvious, he remains impersonal in his narration and never makes any direct value judgment or moral comment on the people or events of his story.

The *Odyssey* has been noted throughout history for the elevation of its thought and diction, the nobility of its speeches and its recurring epithets, and its dignified central theme, derived from the character of Odysseus, who stands alone to conquer fate and successfully triumphs over the opposition of gods, men, and the forces of nature. This emphasis on the experiences and personality of a single great man give it the highest kind of poetic unity. The grandeur and unity of the *Odyssey* are closely interrelated and are the hallmarks of all literary masterpieces. Homer's *Odyssey* is the model which set the standard for all later narrative fiction in western society.

NOTES ON CHARACTERS

HUMAN BEINGS

Aegyptius

One of the chieftains of Ithaca who speaks at the Assembly in Book II.

Agamemnon

The king of Mycenae and leader of the Achaean expedition to Troy; the story of his murder by his wife and her lover on his return home is frequently referred to by Homer, and he is one of the dead souls whom Odysseus speaks with in Hades (Book XI).

Alcinous

The King of the Phaeacians, husband of Arete and father of Nausicaa, he is a generous, kind, and good-humored ruler and father. It is he who makes the return of Odysseus to Ithaca possible.

Antinous

The leader of the suitors and the first one slain by Odysseus in Book XXII. He is a cruel, greedy, and hypocritical villain, always attempting to justify his evil behavior by distorting the motives or acts of others. It is he who first mistreats Odysseus, who constantly harasses Telemachus and Penelope, and who plans the murder of Telemachus. Not only is Antinous malicious, but his evil is so intense that he is unwilling or unable to be ashamed of his deeds and proudly admits them.

Anticleia

The mother of Odysseus; she is encountered by him in Hades in Book XI.

Arete

The queen of the Phaeacians, wife of Alcinous and mother of Nausicaa; in her understanding and kindness she serves as a feminine counterpart to her husband.

Demodocus

A blind bard who entertains at the banquets in the palace of Alcinous. He sings a number of songs, including a humorous one about the love affair of Ares and Aphrodite. His songs about the Trojan War upset Odysseus, and are what eventually cause him to reveal his identity to the Phaeacians. Some readers have conjectured that the portrait of Demodocus is Homer's representation of himself, but there is no proof of this.

Elpenor

A young seaman in the crew of Odysseus who dies in an accident on Circe's island (Book X) and whose spirit reproaches Odysseus in Hades (Book XI).

Eumaeus

The chief swineherd of Odysseus, who remains faithful to his master during his long absence and who plays an active part in assisting Odysseus to regain his position when he finally returns home. He is an intelligent, loyal, and compassionate person, as is demonstrated by many of his acts, among them his kind treatment of Odysseus while he was under the impression that this was only a helpless old beggar.

Eupeithes

The father of Antinous. He manifests the same rashness and disloyalty that is exhibited by his son when, in Book XXIV, he leads a band of Ithacans to attack Odysseus and his party. He is killed in this fight by Laertes.

Euryalus

One of the young Phaeacian noblemen in Book VIII, he brashly taunts and challenges Odysseus but is quick to recognize his error and apologize.

Eurycleia

The faithful and devoted old nurse of Odysseus, who recognizes her beloved master on his return (Book XIX) and who is always willing to serve Odysseus or Telemachus in whatever capacity they require.

Eurylochus

One of Odysseus' officers; he is an unimaginative and sober person, who wisely avoids entering Circe's palace in Book X, but who also abets the sailors when they slaughter Hyperion's cattle in Book XII.

Eurymachus

The second most important suitor; he is as evil as Antinous, but far more soft and cowardly. His instincts are mainly pecuniary and he attempts to appease Odysseus in Book XXII by offering cash restitution for his sins. Unlike Antinous, he is unable to accept the blame for his deeds.

Halisthernes

The soothsayer of Ithaca, who at the Assembly in Book II and at other points in the tale is unheeded when he gives stern warnings of the future consequences of various acts.

Helen

The wife of Menelaus, king of Sparta. She was the cause of the Trojan War in that the Achaeans sailed to Troy to restore her to her husband after she had been, perhaps not too unwillingly, abducted by Paris. Her character here is quite different from that shown in the *Iliad;* she seems a respectable and staid matron, and genuinely sympathetic to the problems of other people.

Irus

A cowardly bully who is a beggar on Ithaca and a favorite of many of the suitors. He is severely beaten by Odysseus in Book XVIII.

Laertes

The old father of Odysseus, who lives in isolation from the demands of public life, on a small farm in the back hills of Ithaca. He remains alert and agile, despite his great age.

Medon

The herald of Ithaca. Although he is forced to serve the suitors, he remains loyal and is spared by Odysseus.

Melantho

One of the serving maids in the palace of Odysseus; she is a nasty and impudent young girl and is disloyal to her master, having become the mistress of Eurymachus. On two different occasions she is needlessly mean to Odysseus, whom she does not recognize, and after he regains power, he has her hung.

Melanthius

The chief goatherd of Odysseus. In his master's absence he has ignored his duty and has ingratiated himself with the suitors by catering to their whims. He assaults Odysseus while he is still incognito (Book XVII) and helps the suitors during the battle in the banquet hall (Book XXII). After Odysseus' triumph, the traitor is executed.

Menelaus

King of Sparta, husband of Helen and brother of Agamemnon. Like Odysseus, he too has a series of misadventures on his return home from Troy (enumerated in Book IV). He is visited by Telemachus (Book IV) and demonstrates indignation at the suitors' behavior and great concern for the young man, but this is clearly a conventional sentiment only, since he offers no real help to the youth.

Mentor

A faithful friend of Odysseus who was left behind in Ithaca as Telemachus' tutor; he is wise, sober, and loyal. Athene often disguises herself as Mentor when appearing among human beings.

Nausicaa

The daughter of Alcinous and Arete. She is a charming young maiden, in her adolescence; her thoughts are occupied only by imaginings of her future husband and by various forms of girlish pleasures and games. She is evidently Homer's portrait of feminine innocence and virtue.

Nestor

King of Pylos, father of Peisistratus. A very wise and garrulous old man, one of the few survivors of the Trojan War. He is visited by Telemachus in Book III.

Odysseus

(Latin: Ulysses) King of Ithaca, husband of Penelope, father of Telemachus, son of Laertes. He is the first of the Greek epic heroes to be renowned for brain as well as muscle; his courage and prowess are beyond criticism, but he is more like a modern than any of the other chieftains who fought at Troy, for he has a sharp and inquiring mind. His mental and physical attributes are of equal importance in helping him to achieve his ends and he uses either, depending upon circumstances. Because he is able to reason and evaluate things, he often hesitates before taking action where other heroes would have rushed blindly into the fray. This must not, however, be interpreted as cowardice. Odysseus' main weakness is his pride, caused by the magnitude of his achievements, and it often involves him in trouble, as when he foolishly identifies himself to Polyphemus and so is subjected to the wrath of Poseidon.

Nonetheless, his courage, wits, and stability enable him to endure all his difficulties and arrive home safely.

Peisistratus

The gallant young son of Nestor. He is the companion of Telemachus on his journey through the Peloponnesus.

Penelope

The wife of Odysseus. She is obviously meant to be a paragon of marital fidelity, having waited twenty years for her husband to return. She is serious and industrious, a perfect wife and mother, but is lacking in the fascination and zest for life that the other women of the *Odyssey* possess.

Philoetius

The chief cowherd of Odysseus; he is brave and loyal and, despite his great age, stands beside his master during the battle with the suitors.

Telemachus

The son of Odysseus. He is just entering manhood and is very self-conscious about his duty, which he is still not fully capable of handling, and his father's reputation as a hero, which he feels he must live up to. His behavior wavers between rash antagonizing of the suitors and brow-beating of his mother, well thought out courses of action like his trip to Sparta and Pylos, complete indifference to goings on around him and shamelessly pathetic appeals to others for aid. It is not until the close of the book, where he shows great courage and steadiness, that one begins to feel that he is, indeed the son of Odysseus.

Tiresias

The most famous of all Greek seers. The legend was that in compensation for his blindness the gods had given him his awesome visionary powers. His spirit is consulted by Odysseus in Hades in Book XI, where he warns the hero of the dangers still awaiting him and predicts his ultimate success and happy life.

Theoclymenus

A fugitive soothsayer who is given passage to Ithaca from Pylos by Telemachus. He warns the suitors of their impending doom in Book XX, but is unheeded.

Argus

The old hunting dog of Odysseus who recognizes his master and dies in Book XVII.

GODS AND SUPERNATURAL BEINGS

Aeolus

A mortal whom Zeus has appointed keeper of the winds. He lives on a mysterious floating island in the western ocean with his wife and twelve sons and daughters. Odysseus' path crosses his in Book X.

Athene

(Latin: Minerva) Daughter of Zeus, goddess of wisdom and patroness of the arts and crafts, also known as Pallas. Odysseus is her favorite and protegé. Although a goddess, she, more than any other female character in the *Odyssey,* is its heroine. She has a leading role in most of the important events, she is nearly always present during the major episodes and her spirit always influences Odysseus and Telemachus. She is the close friend and confidante of Odysseus, and has a sense of humor which is not typical of the Olympian gods. She seems to derive real pleasure and amusement from her relationship with Odysseus, and though the hero has known many women, and has a devoted wife, one feels that only Athene offers him the companionship and understanding of an equal that the modern world expects in a relationship between a man and a woman.

Calypso

The sea nymph who keeps Odysseus captive for nine years and who, in hope of making him her husband, offers him immortality. Her character is not fully developed by Homer, but her presence in the *Odyssey* is possibly meant as a sort of counterpoint of Penelope, whose husband she is able to tempt, but not to snare. Odysseus' adventure with her allows the poet an opportunity for his hero to show his own sense of duty and responsibility, demonstrating that despite his very mortal susceptibility to temptation, he is basically as faithful to his wife as she is to him.

Circe

The enchantress who transforms the crew of Odysseus into swine (Book X) and who, when she finds that she cannot conquer Odysseus himself, takes him as a lover and helps him with advice and supplies on his voyage home.

Hermes

(Latin: Mercury) Son of Zeus, the ambassador of the gods, conductor of dead souls to Hades and patron of travelers, merchants, and thieves. His role in the *Odyssey* is a minor one. He carries Zeus' message to Calypso in Book I; he prepares Odysseus for his meeting with Circe in Book X; and he delivers the souls of the dead suitors to Hades in Book XXIV. His personality is not developed to any extent, and his presence in the epic can be explained on purely functional grounds.

Hyperion

(Also known as Helios) The god of the sun. He travels through the skies each day in a fiery chariot and observes all that takes place on earth. On an island in the western ocean, he keeps several herds of sheep and cattle which are sacred to him; in Book XII, Odysseus and his men land on this island and are punished for the misdeeds they perpetrate there.

Leucothoie

A sea nymph who helps Odysseus to reach the island of the Phaeacians during the storm in Book V.

Polyphemus

A one-eyed giant (Cyclops) who held Odysseus and his men captive in his cave until he was made drunk and blinded by Odysseus (Book IX).

Poseidon

(Latin: Neptune) Younger brother of Zeus, god of the sea and of earthquakes, father of Polyphemus. Because Odysseus is a sailor and must travel home by ship, Poseidon is able to do him much harm. The god bears a grudge against him because of his rough treatment of Polyphemus; however, Poseidon is unable to hold out against the combined pressure of the other gods, of whom Odysseus is a favorite, and so eventually relents.

Scylla

A sea monster with six heads whom Odysseus and his crew must pass during their voyage. Scholars have conjectured that this tale is the result of distorted reports by sailors of giant octopi or squids.

The Sirens

Two beautiful maidens who dwell in a flowery meadow on an island somewhere between that of Circe and the rock of Scylla. They tempt passing mariners to cast themselves overboard and perish on the rocks surrounding their island by singing a tantalizing song, in which they promise to give their victim all sorts of pleasures, and knowledge of all things that have ever happened or ever will happen. (Book XII).

Zeus

(Latin: Jupiter) The supreme god and king of Olympus. He is officially neutral in human affairs; his duty being to carry out the will of Destiny, but he is often sympathetic toward humans. It is he who makes it possible for Odysseus to be aided by Athene, and he ends the civil war in Book XXIV with one of his thunderbolts.

PRINCIPAL GEOGRAPHICAL NAMES

The Achaeans

The Homeric name for the Greek people.

Aeaea

The island home of the enchantress Circe, located somewhere in the unknown western sea (the Atlantic Ocean).

Aeolia

A floating island located somewhere in the unknown western sea (the Atlantic Ocean), the home of Aeolus, king of the winds.

The Cicones

A Thracian tribe whose capital city is raided by Odysseus after leaving Troy.

Hades

The land of the dead in Greek mythology.

Ithaca

The island kingdom of Odysseus, probably located somewhere off the western coast of Greece.

Ismaurus

The capital city of the Cicones, located in Thrace, to the northeast of Greece (modern Bulgaria).

The Laestrygonians

A tribe of cannibal barbarians who seriously defeat Odysseus and his men when the Achaean ships land in their country; their home may have been meant to be located in North Africa.

Ogygia

The island home of the nymph Calypso.

Olympus

A mountain in Thessaly (northeastern Greece), the home of the gods.

The Phaeacians

The inhabitants of the land of Scheria.

Pylos

The kingdom of Nestor, located on the Peloponnesian Peninsula in southern Greece.

Scheria

The island kingdom of Alcinous; the home of the Phaeacians. The location cannot be determined from the information given by Homer and it is evidently meant to be a sort of fairyland, where all people live in peace and prosperity.

Sparta

The kingdom of Menelaus, located on the Peloponnesian Peninsula in southern Greece.

Troy

A kingdom located on the western coast of Asia Minor (modern Turkey) which was destroyed by an Achaean army after a siege lasting ten years.

THE WOMEN OF THE *ODYSSEY*

The *Odyssey* is the product of a society in which the dominant role was played by men. In ancient Greece, just as in the whole of the ancient world, and in America and Western Europe until the last century, women occupied a subservient position. Society was organized and directed by men, and all of the most important enterprises were those which men arranged and implemented. Women were valued, but they participated in the affairs of the world only when they had the tacit or open approval and permission of the men who directed their lives.

The literature of this sort of masculine society, of which the *Iliad* and *Odyssey* are examples, aptly illustrates these social conventions. The themes of these works are subjects which are of interest to men; warfare, hunting, the problems of the warrior and ruler, and so forth. That which would concern women, such as domestic affairs, is not involved in this literature, or is dealt with only casually. Keeping in mind this important attribute of epic poetry, which is the direct result of its social and intellectual environment, one cannot help but note the great difference between the *Odyssey* and all other epic poems. No other literary work of this period, or of a similar cultural background, gives such a prominent position to women. No reader of the *Odyssey* can help having vivid memories of the poem's outstanding female characters. There are many women in the *Odyssey* and all of them contribute in meaningful ways to the development of the action. Furthermore, they are treated seriously and with respect by the poet, as if there were no difference between his attitude toward them and his feelings toward the chieftains for whom his epic was composed. Among the memorable women in the poem are Nausicaa, the innocent young maiden; Arete, the wise and benevolent queen and mother; Circe and Calypso, the sultry and mysterious temptresses; Penelope, the paragon of marital devotion and fidelity; Helen, the respectable middle-class matron with a past; and others, like Eurycleia and Melantho, who have much smaller roles, but equally well defined personalities. Finally, there is Athene, the goddess, who more than any other of these women, has the intelligence, sophistication, and independence that the modern world expects of a woman.

The influential feminine strain in the *Odyssey* also has important effects upon the whole flavor of the poem. Many other early epics are characterized by coldness, morbidity, and brutality, caused by the subjects with which they deal. The virtues, such as courage and martial prowess, which are seen in the *Iliad* are impressive, but they are rough-hewn and limited, for they exist in a world of masculine competition and warfare. It is only in the *Odyssey,* among early Greek works, that such familiar ideas as love, family loyalty, and devotion, and other such important ethical attitudes, are both illustrated and advocated. It is the presence of these unconscious moral lessons that makes the *Odyssey* so unique in its genre and produces its humanitarian and optimistic outlook.

The nature of the events described in the *Odyssey* and the character of Odysseus necessitated that many women had to be present in its verses. Beyond this, however, the poet had a rather free hand in choosing how to deal with them. The women of the *Odyssey* could have been treated as casually and cavalierly as Andromache and Helen were in the *Iliad*. Homer, however, made another choice. In a way, the *Odyssey* is not just the tale of the wanderings of Odysseus. The poet has made it, also, into a sort of "catalogue of women," in which he examines women of all kinds and from all walks of life. These feminine portraits are always objective and fair, for Homer never made judgments, and each of these women has a certain appeal. It is interesting to notice, however, that the woman who is most worthy of respect and emulation is not a mortal. Homer seems to comment that no human being, limited as she was by the evironment which he portrays, could develop herself in this fashion. His admiration for Athene is made even more evident by the fact that she, and not Penelope or one of the others, is the heroine of the poem and the sole companion and confidante of Odysseus. It is only in our modern world that women have been given the opportunity to fully utilize their talent and ability, in order to become equal and contributing members of society like Athene. Understanding this makes a reading of the *Odyssey* even more pertinent to the modern student, for it clearly shows a social problem which has only recently, and still only incompletely, been solved by our world.

THE *ODYSSEY* AND HISTORY

The *Odyssey* is without doubt a valid historical document for an analysis of the institutions and character of the Greeks during an early period in their national development, yet it cannot be of any use until a number of important points and qualifications are made.

All the evidence that has been accumulated through the investigations of archeologists, the probing of later Greek writers, and comparative historical and anthropological studies indicates that the city of Troy did exist and that a war resulting in its destruction did take place, as described in the *Iliad* and the *Odysses*. Furthermore, these studies have also shown that the way of life manifested in the two epics, the forms of government and religion, the attitudes of the people and all the other aspects of the environment are accurate representations of society in what is now called by scholars the "Mycenaean Period" (*ca.* 1400-900 B.C.), named after Mycenae, the most important kingdom of the time.

Beyond these points, it is difficult to make more specific statements. There probably was a real king of Ithaca named Odysseus, around whose name was gathered a whole series of tales, but what his true nature and exploits were can no longer be determined. Many of the adventures described in the *Odyssey* are clearly products of the world of fantasy or the realm of the tall tales told by travelers and sailors. Many of these stories have counterparts in the folklore of other cultures, and similar themes are found in the Near East and the Orient, and in other parts of Europe. As the historical Odysseus developed a reputation, the stories and themes may have become attached to his name, or perhaps Homer was the person responsible for the connection, using his instinct as a poet and teller of tales to merge them into one artistic unit.

If the *Odyssey* is used as an historical document with these things always kept in mind, it can be a valuable source, teaching us what our cultural forebears were like and what sort of world our own has grown from.

SUGGESTED READING

Bassett, S. E. *The Poetry of Homer.* Berkeley: University of California Press, 1938.

Carpenter, Rhys. *Folk Tale, Fiction, and Saga in the Homeric Epics.* Berkeley: University of California Press, 1958 (paperback).

De Vries, Jan. *Heroic Song and Heroic Legend.* New York: Oxford University Press, 1963 (paperback).

Finley, Moses I. *The World of Odysseus.* New York: Meridian Books, 1959 (paperback).

Germain, Gabriel. *Homer.* New York: Grove Press, 1960 (paperback).

Graves, Robert. *The Greek Myths.* Baltimore: Penguin Books, 1955 (paperback).

Hadas, Moses. *A History of Greek Literature*. New York: Columbia University Press, 1962 (paperback).

Kitto, H. D. F. *The Greeks*. Baltimore: Penguin Books, 1951 (paperback).

Lord, Albert B. *The Singer of Tales*. Cambridge, Mass.: Harvard University Press, 1960.

Murray, Gilbert. *The Rise of the Greek Epic*. New York: Galaxy Books, 1962 (paperback).

Nilsson, Martin P. *Homer and Mycenae*. London: Methuen & Co., 1933.

Rose, H. J. *Gods and Heroes of the Greeks*. New York: Meridian Books, 1958 (paperback).

Shewan, A. *Homeric Essays*. Oxford: Clarendon Press, 1935.

Sinclair, T. A. *A History of Classical Greek Literature from Homer to Aristotle*. New York: Collier Books, 1962 (paperback).

Steiner, George, and Robert Fagles, eds. *Homer: A Collection of Critical Essays*. Englewood Cliffs, N.J.: Spectrum Books, 1962 (paperback).

Woodhouse, W. J. *The Composition of Homer's Odyssey*. Oxford: Clarendon Press, 1930.

SAMPLE EXAMINATION QUESTIONS

1. What ancient storytelling techniques influenced the way in which Homer composed the *Odyssey?*

2. Explain: *in medias res,* invocation to muse, epithet, and simile, giving examples when possible.

3. What is known about Homer's life and career? What has been the position of his poetic works in the history of Greece and of western literature?

4. In what ways are the *Iliad* and *Odyssey* similar, and in what ways do they differ?

5. What main themes can be discerned in the plot of the *Odyssey?* How are they given dramatic unity?

6. What aspects of social and political life in Homeric times are reflected in the *Odyssey?*

7. Explain how Homer uses chronology in telling the story of Odysseus?

8. What is the purpose of the many allusions to the legend about the homecoming of Agamemnon?

9. How have the heroes of the *Iliad* changed in the *Odyssey?* How does Odysseus differ from the traditional epic hero?

10. What outstanding personal qualities enable Odysseus to survive all his dangerous adventures and to surmount all obstacles to return home safely and regain his old status?

11. What contradictory tendencies are there in the personality of Odysseus? Why has he often been viewed as a archetypal faustian hero?

12. Discuss some of the ways that have been suggested for interpreting the meaning of the adventures Odysseus undergoes?

13. What is the significance of the visit made by Odysseus to the land of the Phaeacians?

14. Discuss the meaning of the Sirens, Scylla and Charbydis, and Polyphemus.

15. Identify: Circe, Calypso, Alcinous, Poseidon, Nausicaa, Melanthius, Ciconians, Penelope, Antinous, Irus, Argus, Laertes, Nestor, Menelaus, Mentor, Eumaeus, Eurycleia, Helen, Zeus.

16. What role does the goddess Athene play in the *Odyssey?* Why is she often considered its main female character?

17. Why does the pace of the poem slacken after the return of Odysseus to Ithaca and suddenly build up again right before the battle scene in the hall? How is the growing tension alluded to and illustrated?

18. When does the dramatic climax of the *Odyssey* take place? Is this before or after the reunion of Odysseus and Penelope? Why?

19. Discuss such aspects of Homer's style as his objectivity, realism, and compassion.

20. What is the relationship of folklore and fairy tale to many of the stories told in the *Odyssey?* Was there ever a real man named Odysseus?

21. What elements are contained in Book XXIV that are necessary for the story to come to its logical conclusion?

NOTES

*TITLES CONTINUED
ON BACK COVER*

The Study Aid Center for Every Age

CLIFFS TEST PREPARATION GUIDES—complete information for standardized qualification tests in a format that is not overwhelming. The 16 guides in the series utilize the expertise of leading test preparation authorities to help students achieve their best possible test scores. Recommended by counselors and guidance personnel.

Cliffs ACT	Cliffs Math Review	Cliffs GED Mathematics
CBEST	NTE	Reading Skills
ELM Review	PSAT	Science
GMAT	SAT	Social Studies
GRE	TOEFL	Writing Skills
LSAT	Verbal Review	
Essay Exam	Memory Power	

Learn to communicate in a foreign language in "**10 Minutes A Day**" with the **CLIFFS BILINGUAL BOOK SERIES,** and have fun accomplishing what takes years to achieve in a traditional language class. The books make learning an enjoyable family experience. 9 titles available.

Chinese in 10 Minutes A Day	Japanese in 10 Minutes A Day
French in 10 Minutes A Day	Norwegian in 10 Minutes A Day
German in 10 Minutes A Day	Russian in 10 Minutes A Day
Inglés en 10 Minutos al Día	Spanish in 10 Minutes A Day
Italian in 10 Minutes A Day	

A great way to study Shakespeare and Chaucer is provided in **CLIFFS COMPLETE STUDY EDITIONS.** Each book includes the complete text based on the classic Cambridge edition. The unique three-column format includes a running commentary and glossary placed alongside the pertinent text. 12 titles in print.

If you know someone "special," **CLIFFS SPEECH AND HEARING SERIES** can help with information and education problems by acquainting you with the particular area of concern—each of these 13 books contains up-to-date, valuable information for any concerned person.

09218

0   49086 00325   3

Cliffs®
NOTES INC.

Lincoln, NE 68501

ISBN 0-8220-0921-8

THE ODYSSEY